The Resurgence of Nationalism, Racism and White Resentment in the United States of America, Volume I

by

I0408815

Rufus O. Jimerson. Ed. D.

Author of:

- *The Multiracial Legacy of the Roman Empire*. (July 8, 2016). Createspace/Amazon.
- *Africa's Hegemony From Europe's Middle Ages, Its Collapse and Modern Resurgence*. (June 13, 2016). Createspace/Amazon.
- *We Were Kings, Queens, Emperors, Messiahs, Disciples, and Saints*. (May 16, 2016). Createspace/Amazon.
- *The Disproportionate Health Risk of Environmental Racism*. (April 18, 2016). Createspace/Amazon.
- *The "Ferguson Effect" on College Campuses in the United States of America: Protests, Demands, Backlash, and Impact*. (February 12, 2016). Createspace/Amazon.
- *The Holocaust Imposed on The Holocaust Imposed on Black Americans*. (January 14, 2016). Createspace/ Amazon.
- *The Benefits, Beneficiaries and Victims of American Racism*. (October 16, 2015). Createspace/Amazon.
- *He is Not Our Servant: We Are Shepherds of God's Creations, and Not Mere Money Changers*. (September 12, 2015). Createspace/Amazon.
- *Protecting and Serving a Resentful Nation* (August 12, 2015) Createspace/Amazon.
- *When Africa Ruled the World* (July 12, 2015). Createspace/ Amazon.
- *The Impact of New Jim Crow Policing*. (June 10, 2015). Createspace/Amazon.
- *The Crucifixion of President Barack Hussein Obama* (May 6, 2015). Createspace/Amazon.
- *LBJ and the Death of Jim Crow* (April 10, 2015). Createspace/Amazon.
- *Do Black Lives Really Matter? The Prevalence of Repression, Sanctions, and Injustice*. (March 13, 2015). Createspace/Amazon.

ISBN-13: 978-1537480770

ISBN-10: 1537480774

Published by Rufus O. Jimerson, Ed. D,
& Createspace/Amazon

First Edition

Content

Dedicated

To Grandfather, **Theodore Roosevelt Spikes**, who for nearly three decades before his passing, encouraged me to achieve honor and excellence using the pen to articulate ones dreams and visions. He was a Secretary to the Prince Hall Masons for 35 years scripting their secrets like the priest of ancient Egypt. My grandfather took great pride in my academic accomplishments and helped me find the funding needed to realize these achievements. He helped me to develop the paraphrasing writing style that is a dominate tool in over twenty of my books some sixty plus years later.

To Grandma, **Bertha Spikes**, who provided moral and spiritual support, as well as the best tasting meals essential to my ascendency through the wonder years and early adulthood. She partnered with my grandfather to keep me on the straight and narrow using tender love and care.

To Mom, **Mary Estelle Jimerson**, who predicted for five years before her passing that my writings would surpass 30 years of teachings as a value to society. She was an Eastern Star and an enthusiastic and engaged reader.

To Dad, **Rufus O. Jimerson, Sr.**, who experienced a close encounter with two aliens in a dream while being treated as an in-house patient at the Veterans Medical Center, West Palm Beach, Florida.

To my Sisters, **Cynthia and Joyce**, who have aroused from being "Star Children" to become "Renaissance Queens." Cynthia has given the most to "Star Children" and the future of humanity as a committed educator and foster parent.

To My Granddaughter, **Leila Jimerson**, may you be prepared to lead in the footsteps of your father, grandfather, the change agents of the Spikes-Jimerson family, and modern Imhoteps.

To My Grandson, **Malcolm Jamal Jimerson**, may you walk in the footsteps of Jesus Christ, his disciples and your grandfather.

Preface

The purpose of this book is to examine why nationalism, racism and white resentment has spiked during President Obama's tenure. It identifies Donald Trump as the autocrat leading this resurgence. The book reveals the history of nationalism, racism and white resentment since Moors occupied Spain, Portugal and Sicily for more than 700 years. They also became the inbreed progenitors for Europe's royalty, including that of Russia. With the Catholic Church headed by family members, African Moors ruled the less civilized Germanic and Slavic migratory inhabitants for over 1,000 years. The Protestant Reformation and Thirty Year Wars marked the turning point for Europe's black masters and the beginning of a popular revolution by albino masses.

The popular "one man, one vote" constitutional revolution was not completed until 1848 for Western, Central and Southern Europe. From the 17th century's turning point, the Germanic and Slavic descendants of modern Europe not only overthrew the Black Moorish autocratic rule on the continent but extend their rule over Africa, the Americas and Asia. The intergenerational white resentment passed to a grandson of a German immigrant, Donald J. Trump. This resentment among most Euro-Americans has played a devastating role in that harsh treatment experienced by people of color when they were enslaved, assaulted, had their culture, civilization and humanity destroyed while their land and possessions were seized. They imposed a physical enslavement that eventually gave way to a longer neocolonial mental enslavement. In volume 1 of 2, the "arc of justice" is long for people of African descent with no resolution until volume 2. But, history is cyclical and eventually masters or the ruling class will be subordinates to whom they conquer if the subordinates vastly outnumber them as people of color do globally or vice versa by whites in Moorish held Europe.

According to the fair-use rule of the federal copyright law, this book includes images to illustrate points and themes presented that are cited and sourced. Fair use is a limitation and an exception to the exclusive right granted by copyright law to the author of a creative work. It permits the limited use of copyrighted material without acquiring permission from the rights holders. Examples of fair use used in this book include paraphrased interpretations, news reports, research studies and analysis of artifacts, think tank and archive findings and public domain photographic images. Fair use provides for the legal, unlicensed citation or incorporation of copyrighted material in another author's work. Spelled-out is the "fair use" doctrine in Title 17, U. S. Code, sections 107 through 118 of the copyright law.

This book is a copy written analysis and critique of primary sources. Therefore, it is a secondary source. Primary sources are cited. Credit is given to those sources according to citation format recommended by the American Psychological Association's (APA) 5th Manual. This APA formatted inquiry is designed to expand the body of knowledge about subjects identified.

The Resurgence of Nationalism, Racism and White Resentment in the United States of America, Vol. 1

Chapter 1
Resentment Towards Minority/Majority Leadership and
Aspirations in the 21st Century

The Unprecedented Reaction to the Obama Presidency

The resurgence of nativism, racism, Islamophobia and white resentment followed the election of the Barrack Hussein Obama, the first African-American President and a Christian. The Birthers, led by billionaire real estate mogul, Donald Trump, fermented conspiracy theories that the first black president was a secret Muslim who was born abroad and not eligible for that esteem position. For most of the nation's history, our political system was premised on two conflicting facts - one, an oft-stated love of democracy: the other, an undemocratic white supremacy permeating every level of government. Racism placed every Africa-America, including the racially-mixed Obama, under a skeptical eye where they were guilty of wrongdoing, inferior intellect and judgment until they prove otherwise by being "twice as good." The mindset of those obstructing Obama's presidency is that "a black man can't be president in America, given the racial aversion and history that's still out there." An exception to the rule, Barack Obama ended up governing a nation enlightened enough to send an extraordinary, gifted and talented African-American to the White House, but not enlightened enough to accept a black man as its president.

In the wake of the privilege of seeing most sacred cultural practices and tropes of African-Americans validated in the world's highest office, the notion of blacks not being fit for political equality persisted. White communities in the Old Confederacy and in the suburbs and rural areas of the

North and West felt they were entitled to whatever methods or privileges are necessary to prevail, politically and culturally, despite the growing minority demographics. Efforts to discourage minority suffrage and political participation became a higher priority. They felt that the political power, prowess and respectability accorded former presidents must be denied the nation's first African-American president. Once again whiteness, power, status and prestige must be monopolized and reinforced for its own ends. Efforts were stepped up to see that blacks, particularly the most visible ones, like Obamas, must not hold a place of consequence in America's political future (Ibid).

The longed-for post racial moment did not avail itself after Obama won the presidency. Racism intensified as Tea Partiers rallied with signs saying things like "Obama Plans White Slavery (See Image 1)." A favorite of the Tea Party, Congressman Steve King (R-Iowa) complained that Obama "favors the black person." Rush Limbaugh called Obama's presidency a time when "the white kids now get beat up, with the black kids cheering 'Right on, right on'." Glen Beck asserted that Obama had exposed himself as a guy "who has a deep-seated hatred for white people or the white culture... This guy is I believe a racist." White resentment has not cooled off as GOP (Grand Old Party) leaders continue to assert that the black family was better off under slavery rather than wards of the "food stamp president."

Obama has been quite conservative about race. He talked less about this subject than any other Democratic president since 1961. Obama has declined to use his bully pulpit to address racism, instead he sparely used race to rally blacks against their perceived culturally failings. The double standard continues to haunt and constrain the Obama presidency, warning him away from candor about race, hypocrisy and inequitable treatment it manifests (Ibid). His color-blindness is surrender to retrenchment. One man does not make the difference that a social movement does, particularly in a democracy.

Image 1: Tea Party Claims That Obama Plans to Enslave Whites

Source: http://media-files.gather.com/images/d536/d285/d746/d224/d96/f3/full.jpg

A Pragmatic Centrist

Progressives and the left are sincerely disappointed in Barack Hussein Obama. He is not one of them but a pragmatic centrist that has retained the services of numerous Republican bureaucrats and adopted Romney-care as his trademark accomplishment along with more aggressive attacks on terrorist than his predecessor. Irrespective of retaining Republicans and their policies, he has been the focus of a four-year hate campaign funded by Koch Brother and other rightwing billionaires who are donating 1.5 billion to limit him and his party in the U. S. Senate to one term.

The President's biggest legislative target continues to be what conservatives label as Obamacare (Affordable Health Care Reform Act). Mimicked from Romney care that is successful in Massachusetts. This program that transfers taxpayer subsidies to private insurers was created by Koch-funded Heritage Foundation as an alternative to a single-payer health-care plan which is ran directly by the federal government. Ironically, none of the Republicans who previously supported the Affordable Health-Care Reforms created by Heritage Foundation and implemented in the state of Massachusetts actually voted for the act when it was put before Congress. Now, Romney (R-MA) whose program was copied by the Democrats vows to dismantle the federal health care law once he is elected president and is raising millions on disinformation crafted by special interest of big money seeking greater tax cuts and largess (See Image 2). The Roberts-led Supreme Court, which narrowly found the law constitutional, had uprooted over a hundred years of precedents in the *Citizens United* decision to allow corporations to buy our democracy.

The real Obama became the antithesis of being a communist, fascist, socialist, Marxist, Nazi, Muslim, American-hating terrorist or extraterrestrial clone from antiquity (Akhenaten) as the right, including Republican leaders, portrays him through their conservative echo chamber. Nearly the entire moderate Republican leadership has been primaried-out by Tea Party candidates or endorsements. Pragmatic Obama moved to right to the political center. Looking at his record based on the "hope and change," it is disappointing and gives the impression that "he is not even a liberal." Obama ignored liberal and worldwide demands to indict alleged "war criminals" George W. Bush and Dick Chaney or even turn them over to Hague court for trial. The president did ban torture but continued most of the policies related to terrorism and national security adopted by his predecessor. Obama also failed to lead in other liberal causes like same-sex marriage, a single-payer system, and the Fairness Doctrine (Press, 2012).

Image 2: Republican View of Affordable Health Care

Source http://0.tqn.com/d/politicalhumor/1/7/x/q/2/obama-health-reform.gif

To liberals, Obama was a "straw man" whose actions did not match his progressive rhetoric. The reality is that even though Republicans uniformly resisted his initiatives many Democrats are centrist, and some are right of the center to the point whereby any legislation that is too liberal would not pass Democrats, particularly in the Senate. A number of Democrats are members of the Koch-funded Democratic Leadership Council (DLC) once headed by Bill Clinton. Just recently Obama's surrogates who are tied to DLC and Wall Street undermined his re-election campaign against Romney's claim of saving jobs at Bain and Republican opponent's aversion for honesty and other undesirable character flaws.

The real Obama is no knee-jerk Democrats. Recently, he would not campaign for Tom Barrett, Democratic Mayor of Milwaukee, in his failed bid to unseat Republican Governor Walker, who ended collective bargaining in a recall election. Obama was in nearby Chicago, Illinois, fundraising. Back in 2010, he refused to endorse Frank Caprio the Democratic candidate for governor of Rhode Island. Obama chose Lincoln Chafee a Republican colleague he met as a U. S. Senator (Ibid).

Obama also is no Democratic Party ideologue. He sincerely wants and tries hard to govern in a post partisan or trans partisan manner. As a result, he spends considerable time trying to line-up Republican support. To liberals, Obama's efforts look like a waste of his efforts to gain the support of independents that will be needed a close reelection. Obama is perceived as a uniter and consensus builder. Republican leaders, John Boehner (R-OH) and Mitch McConnell (R-KY) responded by making a pledge to make Obama's presidency a failure and limiting him to one term. They would oppose White House initiative, particularly after Republicans gained the House majority in 2010, and any official needed for confirmation other than a Republican or business person.

To the chagrin of progressives, Obama totally caved-in on the Bush tax cuts for the wealthy breaking a campaign promise and rebuking two years of saying that, as president the nation could not afford such a loss in revenue. In July 2011, he surrenders on the debt reduction deal reached with the House's majority. Obama agreed to massive cuts with zero revenue. John Boehner, House majority leader, gloated that he got "98 percent" of what he wanted. Meantime, the president tried hard to convince skeptical Democrats that it was a fair deal (Ibid). Republicans have already reneged on defense cuts by preparing a request in excess of what the Pentagon needs.

Obama's Most Noteworthy Presidential Achievements

Most of what President Obama achieved happened from his inauguration in 2009 to 2010 when Republicans and obstructionist Tea Party politicians become a House Majority. During this timeframe when Obama's initiatives were signed into law the Democratic Party held a majority in the House and Senate, as well as the Executive branch. The four most significant accomplishments of Obama's first term were as follows:

1. Providing hundreds of billions of dollars into infrastructure research and job creation through the American Recovery and Reinvestment Act.
2. Saved American manufacturing by providing loans to Chrysler and GM in order to the preserve auto industry and hundreds of thousands of jobs.
3. Scaled down our ground troops in the Middle East by removing all combat troops from Iraq and significantly scaling them back to training Afghanistan combat troops.
4. To the chagrin of some of the largest financial institutions on the planet pushed for and signed into law an overhaul of the financial markets to prevent another economic calamity (Laessig, 2011).

President Obama achieved a number of significant national security successes over his first term that includes:

1. Signed the New Start Treaty to reduce the nuclear missile stockpiles held by Russia and U. S. by 50 percent.
2. Discontinued Bush's 'global gag rule' to allow American aid to provide family

planning, including abortion counseling to international health organizations.

3. Ordered the assault on Somali pirates who were holding an American ship hostage in 2009 (Ibid).

4. Made the decision to kill Osama Bin Laden, the world's leading terrorist, responsible for 9/11/01 and his network that continues to assault Americans and allies (See Image 3).

The base that elected Obama president was rewarded with the following legislation that favored their special interest as described:

1. For female supporters, the Lilly Ledbetter Fair Pay Act, which made it illegal for employers to pay unequal wages to men and women who perform the same work.

2. For lesbians, gays, transgender, and challenged/disabled, the Matthew Sheppard Act, which expanded the definitions of hate crimes to include gender, sexual orientation, gender identity, and disability.

3. For lesbian and gay community, the Don't Ask, Don't Tell Repeal Act, allows openly gay soldiers to serve in the U. S. military.

4. For university and college students, expanded access to affordable government loans and Pell Grants for college through student loan reform.

5. Disabled and handicapped, dramatically expanded federal efforts into finding a cure for paralysis, as well as increasing support for care and rehabilitation through the Christopher and Dana Reeves Paralysis Act.

6. Hispanics, nominated Sonia Sotomayor, the first Latina, to serve on the U. S. Supreme Court (Ibid,).

Image 3: Killing Bin Laden, Leader of 9/11 Terrorist Attack

Source:
http://upload.wikimedia.org/wikipedia/commons/a/ac/Obama_and_Biden_await_upda
tes_on_bin_Laden.jpg

A number of Obama's achievements universally met the broad base needs of all Americans in medical research, care and insurance, as well as employment, food safety, and debt management as listed:

1. Overturned restrictions on federal funding for stem cell research.
2. Established universal health care for first time in the history of the U. S. through the Affordable Care Act.
3. Provided health care to 11 million children who live in poverty through the Children's Health Insurance Reauthorization Act.
4. Created over 4.3 million private sector jobs.

5. Gave the FDA a mandate in the Food Safety Modernization Act.
6. Outlawed hidden fees and deceptive lending practices from credit card companies through the Credit Card Bill of Rights (Ibid, See Image 4).

What emerges is that Obama is a skillful political player and policy visionaries. He usually seems several moves ahead of his opponent (Fallows, 2012). Obama is directing a definition of Romney, the presumptive Republican nominee, as an ineffective governor (47th in terms of job creation) and profiteer from job and pension raids. All of this skill displayed by Obama will be needed so he can be re-elected for another term because he will be outspent by Romney and Republican 'Super PACs by no less than 400 million. In addition, Republican have used the massive funding edge authorized by Citizen United decision to sweep state legislatures to write voter identification laws that may suppress as many as five million African-American, Hispanic, white student and elderly Democratic votes. Republicans who stole both of George W. Bush's elections are prepared to once again undermine democracy and steal another election.

Obama's Suitability

No one has a presidential experience prior to their first term in office; some have executive experience in either the public or private sector. Obama lacks neither executive and leadership experience nor significant training to do so; therefore, he relies on his instincts and institutional memory of others, particularly from his Clinton appointees. As a result, he became vulnerable to 90s vintage groupthink of these appointees. Obama also led from behind, delegated or let others take the lead in solving problems in their area of competency. He would select the best solution or course of action that others derived somewhat independent of personal investment on his part, direction and intervention if it met

Image 4: President Obama's Major Accomplishments

principles he set forth. Therefore, some Democrats perceived him as an aloof decision maker until a final decision or course of action had to be taken (Ibid).

Obama is perceived as distant and aloof in other matters such as private deals and negotiations. Serene and discipline in public, he seldom demands such from his supporting staff. In the context of predecessors, every president has weaknesses as well as strengths (Ibid). Respectfully, Obama has built probably the most cost efficient campaign with the strongest ground game in the history of the presidency. His experience as a community organizer has helped to build this strength. That ground game may overcome the better funded Romney campaign backed by at least another $600,000 in Super Pac advertisements belittling the Obama presidency.

Unquestionably, President Obama exemplifies an extra high intellectual capacity. Perceived of as a "Mr. Spock" like figure, Obama's emotional reactions do not match that high intellect, ostensibly (Ibid). The brightest and intellectually gifted in the West from the days of the Greeks are taught to be "stoic" and bridal emotions before it interferes with "reason" and "judgment." Expecting people of color to place "emotion" over "reason" and "judgment" is to un-consciously assume they are intellectual interiors and emotionally undisciplined. Since some Democratic representatives and senators stated that he could not relate or connect to them due to not meeting their emotional expectations or being too reserved is really an indictment of their own subtle prejudice. This reason has been used to justify why they would not risk any of their "political capital" to support what is the first "minority-majority" president in a nation where power, money, and privilege have traditionally gone to those of the fairest skin and of obvious European ethnic descent. Conservatives are right in concluding that racism against people of color is as rampant among Democrats as it is among Republicans. The difference is that Republicans have made it a "talking point," agenda and governing policy. The latter is much more humiliating and exclusive than unconscious prejudices that may or may not surface.

Regardless of being "A Man Alone" among Democrats and an open target of Republican prejudice, Obama has grown and adapted in his role of President of the U. S. He has saved the nation from an economic catastrophe initiated by failed policies of the Bush administration (Ibid). Obama broke a promise to his base by bailing-out those in Wall Street that were responsible for the financial collapse and ensuing recession that haunts the economy four years later. In addition, Obama has initiated dramatic improvements in the American image abroad (Ibid). He has scaled back on unilateral actions that created more problems and enemies than solved them. Obama has reinstalled U. S. as a leader in the multilateral approach to foreign policy, isolating enemies and preventing multinational conflicts and wars. To the chagrin of neoconservatives, Obama has reframed from unilaterally intervening in civil unrest and genocide in Syria. Such an action may place the U. S. in an armed struggle with Syria's Russian and Chinese allies and touch-off World War III, Armageddon.

Obama's "Achilles heel" is the recessionary economy he inherited from his predecessor. Romney (R-MA) the former CEO of Bain Capital and Governor of Massachusetts claims that he has the experience and "know how" to fix the economy, reduce unemployment to 6 percent or less and restore American prosperity. In June 2012, the unemployment rate increased from 8.1 to 8.2 percent and Europe the best market for our goods and services is unstable with possible debt defaults in Spain, Italy, and Greece. The "too big, to fail" Wall Street, multinational institutions, are among the biggest creditors for Euro debt along with other financial institutions in Northern Europe. The Federal Depot Insurance makes U. S. taxpayers liable for saving, and checking account held in these banks. These larger banks also are creditors for smaller domestic banks' debts and other businesses that they may have to call-in if their liquidity is saturated by inability of their Euro customers to pay their debts. One or more European national would trigger a worldwide economic collapse. The ripple effect of defaulted loans on our transnational financial institutions would trigger a run on the banks, and another taxpayer bailout could raise the nation's debt threshold by 50 percent or more.

Compounding the threat of national defaults in Europe that would threaten the Euro market and returns on loans from our financial institutions, the Obama administration made some of the following list of mistakes with cumulative economic and political impacts:

- They underestimated the severity of the economic crisis they inherited.
- The solution, stimulus package, was too small to prevent the recession from lingering four years after the financial collapse.
- They were too quick to cover the losses of the Wall Street financers who caused the collapse and much too slow to impose conditions or correctives.
- They spent too much time humoring congressional committees over the health care bill rather than take a lead in its development.
- Did not anticipate that their health care bill would be unpopular today because Democrats in Congress developed the law without the kind of participation by the White House necessary for the administration to effectively sell the package. Someone needed to intervene and say that the bill is too complex for the average citizen to understand

making it vulnerable to misinterpretations by the opposition.

- Obama naively believes that Republicans are willing to set-aside partisan goals for the national interest. Subsequently his admini-stration was slow to recognize the Republican strategy of undermining the president's initiatives by blocking appoint-ments and filibustering bills.
- Adopted the self-destructive Republican claim that the federal deficit was the most immediate threat to the country in the middle of a recession.
- They created a disaster that nearly consumed the nation by trusting that the House majority would responsibly govern and not risk a debt ceiling crisis whereby the federal government would renege on its financial obligations (Ibid).

Regardless of mistakes made, the use of historic numbers of tantrums, filibusters, and other obstructions by the Republicans make the stoic Obama look like the "adult in the room" and rational leader of the nation. If the Tea Party politics continues to run Romney and congressional Republicans "off-the-cliff," the American people will look to the man with the most centrist, pragmatic, caring, and inclusive vision to lead the nation through its slow economic recovery (See Image 5). The best hope of being reelected rest on a majority perception and plurality of votes for President Obama alias Mr. Reasonable (Ibid). Even Mr. Reasonable mistake of being bipartisan to a fault may be an asset to most Americans, particularly to independent swing voters who make a difference in highly contested elections. Regardless of turn weaknesses into strengths, strong precautions must be taken by the Obama administration to prevent Republicans from stealing the 2012 election like they did in

2000 and 2004 by suppressing and undercounting Democratic votes.

Image 5: Winning the Future

From the President Who Happens to Be
Black to Trayvon 'Could Be Me'

On July 19, 2013, President Obama decided to "come out of the closet" and address race (See Image 6). He acknowledges that as a young man, 35 years ago, he could have been Trayvon Martin. His acknowledgement also included that of having been a black teenager, made him a "suspect" and subjected to close scrutiny, being stalked in public places by security personnel, and white women clenching to their bags when he was near them based on his* race. President Obama called for a review of our laws and state officials to neutralize the pain and the prism of racial discrimination and stereotyping brought to the nation's attention by the Zimmerman verdict. Again, he called for respect for the rule of law. This speech was uniquely personal, empathetic and a breakthrough in not only in being a president who is black, but as being the nation's first black president seeking to fulfill King's Dream of an American valuing the content of one's character regardless of race.

At a succeeding press briefing, President Obama acknowledged that all Americans should respect the George Zimmerman verdict, but white America should understand the pain inflicted upon African-Americans from racial profiling and historical that results in a distinct amnesia black experience (Jackson, 2013). He explained that many African-Americans believe that "both the outcome and the aftermath might have been different if Trayvon Martin had been white (Knox, 2013). Americans, particularly those administering our justice system, paint people with a broad brush, Obama points out, and continue to see all black males as potential criminals. As a result, Obama concluded that many African-Americans and other minorities distrust the justice system. Their experience and that of his own provides a prism the views the Zimmerman-Trayvon case through a history where injustice rather than justice prevails (Jackson, 2013).

Image 6: A President Taking on the Toxic Subject of Racism and Unequal Justice

Source: http://news.yahoo.com/-obama--trayvon-martin-%e2%80%98could-have-been-me-35-years-ago%e2%80%99--180734663.html

The reality, Obama points out, is that African-American males are both "victims and perpetrators" of crimes. They are more likely to harm themselves and those living in their own communities. He left out the fact that they are over policed and this phenomenon has resulted in a higher arrest rate. Obama also implied rather than indict a failed justice system for the higher convictions and the role overworked and ill-prepared public defenders, as well as prosecutors seeking higher rates of convictions by offering plea bargains that generated higher incarceration rates. He also did not clarify how black males are disproportionately arrested for drug use. Obama did suggest that to insure that the role of race in law enforcement and the justice system is reduced and changed states should primarily review the use of deadly force. In conjunction, he suggested that Americans should push for Conyers (D-MI) bill prohibiting or reducing profiling and a program involving the Justice Department and governors that could provide law enforcement training designed to reduce "the kind of mistrust in the system that sometimes exist (Volsky & Millhiser, 2013).

Obama in his address on race and Zimmerman-Trayvon verdict, points out that all black males are subjected to being followed by security guards while shopping, motorist locking their doors upon their presence and women tightly holding their purses in an elevator or as they walk by, including himself prior to being a senator (Jackson, 2013; Knox, 2013; CNN, 2013; Sala & Sala, 2013). The president stated that state and local governments should examine how they could reduce violent confrontations rather than encourage citizens to shoot suspects based on perceived fear. In addition, law enforcement agencies, he suggests, need to use racial sensitivity training to reduce tensions between police and minorities. Obama holds that Florida's "stand your ground" law encourages confrontation, racial pain and schism (Jackson, 2013). He believes that it is a national imperative to restore the trust of all Americans in the judicial and law enforcement system.

This speech is the first time Obama has admitted that the nation is not a post-racial society and that racism is pervasive today. His solution to the racial divide made evident by the Zimmerman acquittal includes introspection between citizens at the familiar and community (church) level as opposed to a national conversation. The citizenry, as he sees it, should appeal to their "better angels" to close the divide. Obama recognizes that over the course of decades, American race relations have improved. He acknowledges that the nation had become better for all but it still has a long way to go to become a perfect union (Ibid). In this regard, the President Obama asked that the nation to do more to give African-American boys "a sense that their country cares about them and values them and is willing to invest in them"

(Sala & Sala, 2013). In effect, he has appealed to the nation to fulfill King's Dream started nearly 50 years ago. Yet, it is unclear that a nation with a tradition of democracy, slavery and racism would fully pursue the rights and freedoms of the descendants of the slaves in the waking of the rise of a new minority-majority that is predominantly non-white or black and brown.

Manufactured Crisis of Competence

Besides using racial innuendos to undermine the leadership of the first Afro-American president, the Republicans and their rightwing constituency manufactured numerous crises to nullify President Obama's initiatives, influence, and power. One of the most effective manufactured crises tied to the president is that of Ebola and its exaggerated threat to the health of the nation. President Obama is being blamed for the spread of this fear and subsequent hysteria. A crisis of confidence has been created in his is and the federal government's competency (Thiessen, 2014).

The crisis of competency was heightened by the revelation that an Ebola-infected doctor, Craig Spenser, traveled extensively in NYC. He took a three-mile run, visited a coffee stand, ate at a restaurant, traveled on three subway lines, met friends at a Brooklyn bowling alley, etc., in one of the most highly populated city in America. Spencer traveled in the public without violating the government's Ebola protocols. According to protocols, a health worker is advised to see a doctor if his or her body temperature reaches 100.4, limit contact with other people and avoid public transportation. In contrast, the white governors of New York and New Jersey stepped in and imposed their own 21-day mandatory quarantine on health-care workers returning from areas in West Africa where they treated Ebola patients (Ibid).

As a result of outcries from the rightwing "outrage machine," Americans dramatically lost their faith in the Center of Disease Control (CDC) and trust in the president's leadership. Polls indicate that only 37 percent of the Americans sampled today believe that the government is doing a good or excellent job. Back in May 2013, 60 percent felt that the government did a superlative job in containing diseases like Ebola. Obama was polled by a 58 percent majority as incompetent in managing the federal government. Charges included the botched Obamacare rollout, the border crisis, the VA scandal, IRS scandal, the General Services Administration scandal, etc. The latter poll was conducted by Fox News, a principle enabler of the rightwing "outrage machine" (Ibid).

The crisis of competency became a mid-term issue that catapulted Republicans into control of the Senate, House and control of state governments. Prior to this triumph, at least a dozen Democrats in close races set themselves apart from Obama over his management of the Ebola crisis. Only 22 percent of the likely voters polled expressed 'a lot of confidence' that the government is doing everything it can to contain the spread of Ebola. Another 31 percent said that they have no or little confidence in the government's management of the situation, so far. Vulnerable Democrats have been nearly as critical as the Republicans in questioning the president's and government's competency in this respect (Chambers, 2014).

Amid assurances on Ebola, President Obama convened his top aides in respect to this crisis on the fatal disease. He demanded that his aides get ahead of events and take a more hands-on approach, especially in respects to the CDC. The responses were considered less than satisfactory. The Ebola crisis became the latest event that stretched his national security staff thin prior to the midterm. Simultaneously, ISIS' military campaign was escalating, the specter of a new Cold War with Russia was evolving over Ukraine, and Yemen, a seedbed for Al Qaeda, was disintegrating (Shear & Landleroct, 2014).

Judicial Watch (JW), another enabler of the rightwing "outrage machine," claims that President Obama plans to circumvent existing laws and regulations to bring Ebola victims into the states within days of diagnosis. In addition, JW claims that the president intents to circumvent the constitution and legal precedents to clear a path for citizenship for millions of illegal aliens. His immigration czar portends that some 130,000 undocumented children would cross the border. JW also frowned upon the president's appointment of an Ebola Czar who is not an expert in infectious diseases. They point out that the White House sees Ebola as more of a political crisis than a threat to public safety (Judicial Watch, 2014).

Talk about Obamacare, the inequality gap, education, energy policy or the country's sagging infrastructure were supplanted by the politics of escalation to keep Americans safe. The demand for more planes, drones, bombs, special ops forces, advisors and boots on the ground to combat ISIS and Ebola took over the midterm (Engelhardt, 2014). The right wing's "outrage machine" backed by the "Industrial-Military Complex" drove this issue in respect of their interests. They defined "competency" as the ability to fully fulfill their demand. This placed enormous pressure on the Obama administration who were confronted by conservative Democrats struggling to retain their Senate seats.

The midterm elections became a referendum on Obama's leadership (See Image 7). His and government's perceived incompetency in regards to Ebola and Foreign Affairs rallied the far right. Democrats abandoning their President, his policies, and the new voter identification requirements suppressed the Democratic vote. As a result, Republicans recaptured control of the US Senate and picked up additional seats in the House of Representatives. The House majority became the biggest since the Hoover administration. In addition, Republicans picked up governorships in the blue states of Illinois, Maryland, and

Massachusetts to further hamper Democratic votes in the 2016 presidential election (Bowman & Pessin, 2014).

Image 7: The 2014 Midterm That Mummified President Obama

Source: www.nybooks.com

Democrats blamed the Republican capture of the Senate on two enemies who were not even on the ballot, namely (1) unruly Tea Party and its primary election purges and (2) a $2 billion campaign attacks associating Democrats in swing states with unpopular President. Yet many of these conservative Democrats in the Hillary Clinton camp privately agree with Republicans that Obama's competency in office is questionable at best. These perceptions are in contrast to the more disciplined, effective, campaigns of the Republicans that received unlimited "dark money." Obama was denied invitations by Democrats in these swing states to defend his record. Obviously, this operational failure led to the overwhelming defeat of swing state Democrats and party's control of the Senate.

The Resurgence of Nationalism, Racism and White Resentment in the United States of America, Vol. 1

Chapter 2
How White Resentment Broke the Political Culture and Consensus

A Nation Divided by Race

Race and how politics protected and promoted white privilege and supremacy marked this nation from its founding. Up until 1850 Compromise that allowed western states to come into the union as free states, Southern interest based on white supremacy, privilege and African slavery dominated the aim of the nation's laws, Congressional representation, national security and executive leadership. Most of the presidents of this new nation were slaveholders. Slaveholders dominated the US Senate and the rest of the Congressional leadership. But slave labor hampered the industrial development of the North and acquisition of natural resources to feed the engines of factories and technical development. Moral dissent wed with this economic outlook along with a vision of transforming the nation into a world-class superpower. The original Republican party was established to achieve this visionary "Manifest Destiny." The obstacle to its growth was a government and its political institutions devoted to the expansion of slave labor that hampers the economic development needed for a world-class industrial power.

The Western nations led by the British global empire had quickly proceeded through an Industrial Revolution. The Brits vast mercantile system locked American trade out of its colonial markets. The same systems were instituted by France and Spain. Unless, from the point of view of the Republican "free traders," Americans could expand the free labor market and its pool of higher skilled Europeans, it could not compete with world-class industrial nations and would be delegated to economic underdevelopment.

The election and reelection of President Barrack Hussein Obama amplified white male resentment and fear of a minority/majority takeover of their democracy. Since Democrats passed the civil rights and voting rights laws in the 1960s, the white vote, especially older men in the former Confederate states have joined the GOP's camp. Reagan Republicans offered them white resentment policies designed to put blacks and browns in their so-called place "beneath the feet" of whites in the bottom of society. To do so, the Republican continues to press for legislation and rulings that would void affirmative action, the black vote, federal efforts to mitigate poverty, investments in infrastructure and education in black and brown communities and so forth (Williams, 2015).

The Obama presidency has spawned a period of heightened racial animus and terrorism against people of color. The best example of the racial extremism invoked was the actions of Dylann Roof a 21-year old white male. He murdered nine people worshipping at Charleston's Emanuel African Methodist Episcopal Church. Roof was motivated by a delusion that the murder of six women and three men would precipitate a race war, avenge the rape of white women and prevent blacks from taking over the government from white men (Richardson, 2015). Blacks are not unified by race like whites. They are more likely to get upset about offenses to blacks in their own socioeconomic class. Those in the lower or underclasses are more likely to resort to violence if one of their own is publically abused. Their violence is likely to target the material objects that are normally beyond their means. They would either destroy them or steal them for illegal sales. Church goers are normally considered members of the middle class. Their black counterparts are more likely to use nonviolent means incumbent in the political system to address their grievances. This insightful information was well beyond the awareness of low information, bigoted, white males like Dylann Roof.

Roof stated that "he had to do it," murder nine Church going blacks because these people "rape our women and they are taking over our country." His statements and bigoted mindset derives from white Southern males unable to grip with the fact that they would no longer control the country. Roof and his cohorts were reminded of this fact when a black man was elected to the presidency and was reelected to the highest office for a second time. Similar to the first Reconstruction, they reinstitute terror and murder to prove that white males are still beyond the law and superior to blacks. They yearned for the days that if caught, no all-white jury would find them guilty despite the amount of evidence. Back in the good old days, when American was great, few white men would dare to testify to protect blacks and blacks would not be believed or considered credible.

The Roots of White Southern Resentment

In antebellum America, Southern Democrats controlled the nation's politics. Government was used to prop up the system of racial slavery that enriched white men. Northern whites organized themselves to contain the spread of this Southern system. The Northerners under the banner of the Republican party insisted that every man should have a say in how they are governed. Once in power, they used the government to promote self-determination and industry (Ibid).

Under Republican led government during and after the Civil War, white Southerners refused to face the reality of sharing power with blacks. This meant obstructing federal efforts to give poor men land, education and freedom if it included sharing these benefits and governance with the former slave. Southerners used state's rights to enforce "Black Codes" that would legally place blacks back into bondage by denying them their freedom and access to economic, political or social power. Under the code, blacks could not own guns, were required to sign year-long contracts or face arrest as "vagrants" and were bound to anyone who paid their fines. They also could not testify in court against a white person and, in effect, claim the protection of the law against theft, rape and murder (Ibid).

The Reconstruction Era Republicans refused to accept placing African-Americans into a quasi-slavery status that would place the cost of war on the Union after the Confederacy spent four years trying to destroy the nation. They, in turn, made readmission to the Union contingent on accepting the Fourteenth Amendment giving black men legal rights and "due process." Southern whites opted for a military occupation rather than submit to black legal equality. In 1867, northern congressmen passed the Military Reconstruction Act calling on Southern states to rewrite state constitutions providing for black civil rights, including male suffrage. Under this act, Republicans were able to organize black voters. White southerners in return refused to enroll black voter (Ibid).

Congress placed the army in charge of voter registration. White southerners organized the Ku Klux Klan as a vigilante force to stop the change of government. Prior to 1868 elections, at least a thousand African-Americans and white allies were murdered by the Ku Klux Klan. But, black voters, primarily in the South, helped to put Republican Ulysses S. Grant in the White House. Klan terrorism accelerated after the election. Whites howled that black voters were taking over the country similar to what the cat-called in the 21st century when Obama was elected as the nation's first black president. In 1871, under a law making political intimidation a federal offense, President Grant was able to impose martial law through federal courts to try 1,000 offenders. White southerners continued to step up their efforts to silence black voices and political empowerment. Then and now, white southerners insisted that blacks only wanted social welfare legislation that would enable them to live without working. They argued that the programs from the legislation would redistribute tax dollars from hardworking white men 'corrupting' the government and destroying America itself (Ibid).

Relevance to the Obama Presidency

In the reaction to Obama's presidency and reelection, Fox News, talk radio hosts, movement conservatives and Reagan Republican have stoked the Reconstruction fears that they are losing control of the government to freeloading blacks and "47 percent" who are seeking handouts like free health care, food, housing, etc., (Ibid). This assertion is led by enablers of the right such as Rush Limbaugh, Glen Beck and Ted Nugent who have gained enormous riches and attention by scapegoating Obama and blacks for all of the nation's ills. Limbaugh has pushed the line that Obama, Oprah Winfrey and Eric Holder have gained their esteem only because they are black. Beck pushes the line that Obama has a "deep-seated hatred for white people or white culture," irrespective of being a product of a white mother. Ted Nugent, Conservative icon and former rock star has been on a campaign of calling Obama a "subhuman mongrel" (Dees, 2014).

It has become evident that during the Age of Obama, America's political culture is broken. According to a Pew Research Foundation report there is empirical evidence substantiating this break. Liberal and conservatives are significantly polarized regarding the need for racial and ethnic diversity. The Left and Right cannot find a realistic common ground. Movement conservatives have refused to seriously consider the problem with guns purchased by the mentally ill and terrorists on the no fly list. In addition, they refuse to give any ground on global warming and many areas of scientific research. Facts and the truth seems to be oblivious to movement conservatives (De Vega, 2014).

There is no agreement between liberals and conservatives on the nature of the common good and the role to be played by the social compact in American life (Ibid). Freedom defined by movement conservatives means reserving the choice to live in segregated communities in white homelands controlled by their state and local governments, free of federal laws, rules and regulations. They are appealing to tribal feudalism rather than maintain a strong modern "world-class" democratic government that serves all of its people regardless of race, ethnicity, gender and religion.

Movement conservatives and their nativistic following are anxious about the "browning of America" from the nation's changing demographics. They are afraid that whites will no longer be a majority in the United States. Movement conservatives see the Democratic Party who are best at representing the interest and needs of the "others" as threatening to impose a minority/majority rule. They see themselves as best representing the identity politics of the Republican party and traditional white majority. During the Age of Obama, the Tea Party arose among these movement conservatives. They primaried-out moderates and liberal among the ranks of Republican lawmakers and executives. Using identity politics, the Tea Party aroused racial animus toward the "other" and transformed the Party's political policies into practices aimed at creating an Apartheid government.

White supremacy and right-wing propaganda have created a state of racial, ethnic, and gender derangement, as well as Islamophobia, among conservatives. This derangement is evident in their birther madness, Benghazi obsession, "death panels," embracement of neo-confederacy, swastika proliferations, talk of nullification, domestic terrorism and unprecedented lawsuits challenging Obama's executive orders as violation of "checks and balances" between branches of the government. The election of Barrack Obama activated "old-fashion racism" and white resentment to impair consensus and elevate partisanship to an undesirable extent. The reaction has also shattered the illusion that America is now a "post-racial society" or has moved "beyond race."

The Republican party is now dedicated to destroying the legitimacy of the federal government. They are trying to abolish or diminish the "safety-net" which disproportionately protects blacks and browns at the margins of the socioeconomic system. Conservatives see them as "useless eaters" and "stealing" the resources of hardworking white Americans. They ignore their 1 percent donor class that live off corporate welfare and a rigged tax code that enables them to extract far more wealth and resources than they contribute (Ibid). This is why Donald J. Trump, the billionaire presumptive nominee of the Republican Party, refuses to display his tax returns, allegedly they may show he paid little to no taxes whatsoever. The return may also show he is reluctant to give to charities compared to the Clintons and many other Americans with comparable or less wealth.

Another survey suggests that scapegoating the diverse cultures of blacks and browns for the loss of cultural dominance has become commonplace. These traditional whites feel that cultural changes favoring people of color have come at their expense. They are nostalgic for the 1950s when the culture they were exposed to in a highly segregated America was exclusively white with few exceptions. They are angry about this multiculturalism which celebrates cultures and people whites traditionally considered inferior or subhuman. These traditional whites feel that multiculturalism that diminishes their cultural hegemony is discriminatory towards them and therefore makes them victims even though this notion is illusionary (Morse, 2016).

Mainstream society's cultural dominance has slipped. Latinos are gaining hegemony. The Black Lives Matter movement is gaining momentum. Unquestionably, the Pan-African Movement is drawing a large following on the worldwide web. Simultaneously, whites without a college education have loss good paying jobs to labor markets in the

Third World (South of the Border, Africa, Asia and Pacific Rim) and to technological advances. The resentful white working class has turned their anger on the less privileged blacks and browns instead of blaming the donor class that control the Republican Party. The donor class, irrespective of party affiliation, have moved record number of jobs to other shores to maintain their hegemony on profits. By funding enablers of xenophobia and racism they inundate low-information Americans with misconceptions, conspiracies, easy answers, hubris and notions of entitlement that are "out-of-touch" with their own interests. They are fooled into believing that their absent of color makes them superior and entitled to wealth and sociopolitical status over "others" with more melanin.

Unprecedented Obstruction Confronted by the Nation's First Black President

To the condemnation of right-wing pundits, former Attorney General Eric Holder suggested that racial animus played a role in the level of vehemence and obstruction encountered by President Obama. Holder called out the Republican leadership for partisan collusion to sabotage the presidency of the first African-American head of state (See Image 8). The racism described by Holder was obvious since the 2008 campaign. Obama was mischaracterized as a Muslim, Kenyan, communist dictator or tyrant, racist and terror sympathizer (Dees, 2014). Today in 2016, Donald J. Trump, the Republican Party's presumptive nominee for the presidency has suggests that Obama is sympathetic to the ISIS terrorists because he would not identify them as "Islamic terrorist," commit war crimes like torture against them and take revenge on their families and the billions following Islam. Interestingly, his 16 million followers and America's white majority have never labelled white terrorists, like Dylann Roof and the Klan as "Christian terrorists" who want to preserve white, Christian, dominance.

Image 8: Unprecedented Presidential Obstruction

Republicans Just Say No ... to Everything

Bill	Signed	Senate Vote	GOP Votes	House Vote	GOP Votes
S-CHIP	Feb 2009	66-32	8	290-135	41
Stimulus	Feb 2009	60-38	2	246-183	0
Health Care Reform	Mar 2010	60-39	0	219-212	0
Wall Street Reform	Jul 2010	60-39	3	237-192	3
Extended Unemployment Benefits	Jul 2010	59-39	2	272-152	31
Small Business Jobs Act	Sep 2010	61-38	0	237-187	1
DISCLOSE Act (filibustered)	---	59-39	0	219-206	2

Source: www.dailykos.com

The election of Obama has resulted in an explosive growth of radical-right groups, including armed militias and repeated threats that violence is needed to "take our country back" from the tyranny of our black "other" ruler and leftist supporters. This racial resentment is continually ginned-up by Republicans and right-wing media machine with coded words. This resentment has been ginned-up since Nixon implemented the "Southern Strategy" to enhance the white backlash after the triumphs of the civil rights movement. The racial animus used to gain the presidency and congressional majorities in the House of Representative and Senate for the Republicans since Nixon was updates and aimed at President Obama. It resulted in a record-setting political obstruction designed to minimize or neutralize the effectiveness of the first African-American president. None of Obama's economic incentives to promote job growth since the stimulus bill at the beginning of his first term have reached his desk from a Republican-controlled Congress. As a result, the economic recovery has been prolonged and growth and job rates have been relatively stagnant compared to other comparable periods.

The Obama administration faced a record-setting usage of the filibuster (See Image 9) and united fronts against his legislative agenda to blocking judicial nominees and threats to trigger a US default. This total obstruction of the president's agenda was called for by conservative think-tanks and right-wing pundits prior to Obama's oath of office. On inaugural night, fifteen top Republican leaders met to execute this plan to sabotage the new president from the start of his first term. Led by the likes of Paul Ryan these leaders schemed to challenge every single bill introduced by the Obama administration (Perr, 2012).

Image 9: Republican Usage of the Filibuster

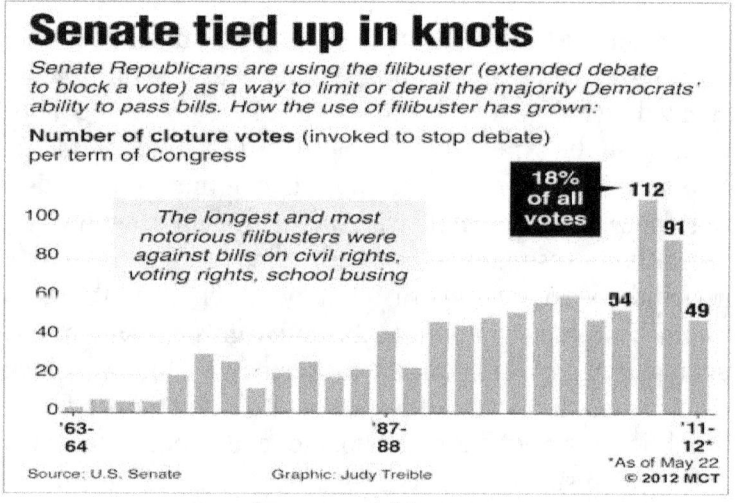

Source: www.dailykos.com

From the inauguration night, Obama's legislative agenda ran into endless Republican obstacles in Congress. His judicial nominees failed to get a hearing and Senate confirmation vote. The Senate confirmed fewer district and circuit nominees than every president since Jimmy Carter and at the lowest percentage of any president in American history during their first term (See Images 10-11). Judicial standouts never experienced a hearing or if so, a vote.

Administrators were simultaneously blocked from a confirmation hearing and vote, particularly during Obama's second term (Ibid).

Image 10: The Senate's Confirmation of Judicial Nominees

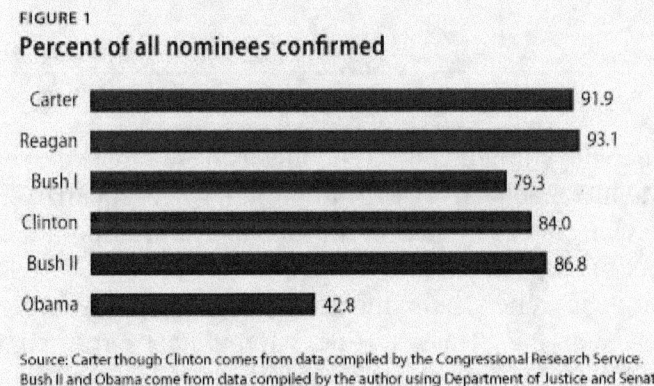

Source: www.dailykos.com

Image 11: Percentages of Nominees Confirmed

FIGURE 1
Percent of all nominees confirmed

President	Percent
Carter	91.9
Reagan	93.1
Bush I	79.3
Clinton	84.0
Bush II	86.8
Obama	42.8

Source: Carter though Clinton comes from data compiled by the Congressional Research Service. Bush II and Obama come from data compiled by the author using Department of Justice and Senate Judiciary Committee information.

Source: www.dailykos.com

In 2014, Republicans blocked every serious idea to strengthen the middle class. The Senate filibustered hundreds of bills since 2009 and anything that might help the economy. The only thing not obstructed was tax relief for the wealthy and corporations (See Image 12). They cut spending on essential things like maintaining our infrastructure and scientific research. Republicans also cut regulations that protect people and the environment from harm to enhance corporate donations to their campaigns from the world's leading polluters (Johnson, 2014).

Image 12: Economic and Health Care Assistance Versus Tax Relief for the Rich

The Republican One-Way Street:
Bipartisan Support for Health Care, Stimulus and Tax Bills

	Obama	Obama	Clinton	Bush	Reagan
Year	2010	2009	1993	2001	1981
Bill	HCR	Stim	Tax/Stim	Taxes	Taxes
Amount ($ Billions)*	$940	$787	$496	$1,350	$749
Senate Votes	56	60	51	58	89
- Democrats	56	57	51	12	37
- Republicans	0	3	0	46	52
House Votes	220	246	218	240	323
- Democrats	220	246	218	28	133
- Republicans	0	0	0	212	190

Source: www.dailykos.com

Since the stimulus bill, Republicans have blocked every effort to hire teachers, raise the minimum wage, equalize pay for women, stop tax breaks for millionaires and corporations, stop tax breaks for sending jobs out of the country, provide student loan relief, help the long-term unemployed, and more. Using the "Hastert Rule," Republicans refused to bring a bill up for vote unless a majority of their rank support it. This is why common sense gun control has not passed regardless of the record number of lone wolf terrorist massacres including the recent mass murder of people in Orlando at the night club patronizing gays. The budget passed by Republicans is designed to slowly sabotage the economy and procure the perception that it is headed in the wrong direction under Obama and future Democratic leadership (Ibid).

The Resurgence of Nationalism, Racism and White Resentment in the United States of America, Vol. 1

Chapter 3
Donald Trump's Neo-Nationalist and Xenophobic Movement

The Rise of Donald J. Trump, Racial Animus and Intolerance

In mid-June 2016, Trump is the presumptive presidential nominee of the Republican Party as the "No Trump" movement failed to generate a contender and the "ground swell" of Republicans to challenge the primary winner. The latter movement is trying to pass a rule allowing convention delegates to follow their conscious rather than represent primary voters who sent them to Cleveland to select Trump as the Party's presidential nominee for the fall election. Trump is facing a rebellion of establishment Republicans concern about Trump's electability and adherence to principles. Trump has effectively alienated many Americans by his xenophobic, racist and misogynist insults minus specifics to improve the economy and jobs in a manner that would not force the nation into bankruptcy. Establishment Republicans for more than a decade have welcomed blacks, browns, women, religious minorities, gays, etc., under the banner of its conservative principles, particularly in regards to the general election. Those principles produced token, cosmetic and exclusionary policies and practices contrary to a meaningful inclusion of a wider and more diverse base. Trump, an alleged multibillionaire and exponent of unprincipled white rage and bigotry, has beaten sixteen more inclusive and principled competitors for the nomination. Ironically, Trump won the primary votes of a Republican minority, primarily Tea party white nationalist, in the highly diverse field of candidates, yet over 80 percent of the Republicans polled support his selection but as Hillary

Clinton, the Democratic presumptive nominee, gains a double-digit lead, a majority of GOP voters want another nominee.

At this point prior to the Republican Convention on July 18-21, 2016, Trump will likely be confirmed the Republican presidential nominee unless there is a massive rebellion of consciousness and fear that Trump's bid at the top of the ticket will cause down ballot Congressmen and governors to massively lose to Democrats. The "No-Trump" Movement is making that point as Trump is beginning to significantly fall behind Hillary Clinton in polls, particularly in swing states, like Florida. Trump's brazen bigotry has caused donors to deny him contributions and redirect their donations to down ballot Republicans. As a result, the Clinton team has amassed a $22 million advertisement buy to reverse her right-wing imposed negatives promoted by well-funded Republican donors and conservative enablers. Without enough financial contributions, Trump has not bought any contradictory ads to date. Therefore, the Clinton campaign and Democratic political action committees have a head start lead on defining their nominee and maligning Trump and the Republicans.

Trump's rise to the presumptive nomination is a creation of the Republican Party's appeal to the white working class for a government that would widen the socioeconomic status between them and up-incoming nonwhites. Republicans since they recruited Dixiecrats into their ranks have blames minorities for why the white working class has declined in status and perceived political clout. Simultaneously, the Republicans have brought together conservative measures funded by affluent donors to produce policies and laws to elevate the 1 percent donor class, freeing them of taxes, regulations and helping them reinvest in jobs abroad for higher returns. In exchange, a record number of employers and their revenues are now offshore making alleged billionaires like Trump super billionaires. Trump, an offshore predator, has promised to reverse this trend through the persuasion of his own personality or import tariffs taxes on offshore goods in exchange for the white working class vote needed to become the president. He seems to be ignorant of or ignore the fact that his political party is in control of the House and Senate by virtue of campaigns funded by donors reaping huge returns from the offshore holding the presumptive nominee promises to stop if he is voted into the oval office.

One of the foundational principles of the Republican party is "free trade." Democrats stood for high tariffs against imports to protect its budding manufacturing jobs in "rust belt" where coal was extracted and steel produced, as well as the textile factories of New England. These jobs produced a thriving middle-classes on the bases of a high school education and on-the-job training. The Democratic Party held the majority of the white vote from this manufacturing base and the solid Jim Crow South until President Johnson approved the civil and voting rights bills in the mid-1960s. The "free trade" Republican Party used the "Southern Strategy" under President Reagan to effectively appeal and maintain the support of the nation's white majority to today. Bill Clinton reorganized the Democrats from a party relying on its liberal base to one attractive to centrist Americans by appealing to "free trade" as a means to enormous economic growth while limiting federal expenditures to achieve a balanced budget. The outsourcing of manufacturing and textile jobs was further spurned by Republican President George W. Bush to offset a deficit he incurred by his misdirected wars on Iraq and Afghanistan. President Obama was left with a stagnant economy where financial institutions were called on credit and loans most Americans depended upon to offset the loss of purchasing power based on a shrinking salary and job base due to accelerated investments and lucrative returns from offshoring and automating jobs. The next president will have to decide whether they will enter the Trans Pacific Partnership or concede Southeast Asia to Chinese hegemony. Trump has promised to renegotiate all these deals to recover these jobs or penalize importers of imports and therefore spurring record inflation and trade war hurting American consumers unless he contracts all his promises or face unpopular, bipartisan obstruction, more rigged than his predecessor. Trump would then be more likely to manufacture another holy war like Bush and renege on the national debt to bankrupt and destroy the American way of life.

Trump's message is similar to the pre-civil rights Democrats appeal to working class white voters prior to outsourcing of manufacturing jobs wage stagnation due to cheaper labor offshore and immigration domestically that have skyrocketed in recent decades. Economic insecurity is a root cause of Trump's appeal. But racial attitudes, including racial resentment and explicit racial stereotypes, are the most important factor in his appeal. Fan's flock to him as a result of his racist, white nationalist sentiment. Trump won the Republican primary by appealing to racial intolerance at a greater extent than his sixteen other competitors (See Image 13; McDaniel & McElwee, 2016).

Racism today tends to be more than less subtle. Practitioners tends to use "dog-whistles" and stereotypes that appear as neutral but still animate racial anger. The Republican Party since Reagan have run on "dog-whistle" racism. This racism emphasizes racial resentment. Blacks the most frequent targets are responsible for their own disdain because according to Trump and his supporters these "others" or "those blacks" should:"

- Work their way up without special favors
- If they would only, try harder they could be just as well-off as whites.
- They have gotten more than they deserve because of affirmative action based on racial preferences (Ibid).

Support for Trump increased along with racial animus. Trump support heightens with those that believe that black people, Muslims and Hispanics are "lazy" or "violent." This support evolved from the racial animus seeded by Reagan's "Southern Strategy" or white resentment movement. It began with Reagan decrying "welfare queens" evolved to Rick Santorum's "I don't want to make black people's lives better by giving them somebody else's money" through numerous GOP leaders using racially-charged rhetoric to sabotage support for the social safety not. This evolution in racial animus empowers a demagogue like Trump (Ibid).

Image 13: Trump's Call for Intolerance

Source: www.nationalreview.com

Racial resentment stands at the core of Trump's campaign and nativist movement (See Image 14). He launched his campaign by painting Mexican immigrants as rapist and drug dealers (Reifowitz, 2016). Interestingly, Mexicans, particularly his targeted illegals, are less likely to commit crimes that would get them deported and unable to complete the labor needed to meet the financial needs of their families South of the border. Mexicans are more American than European-Americans that follow Trump. They descend from American Indians more than Spaniards and African slaves. Mexicans do represent what is considered the browning of America and are perceived as a threat to the Anglo-American mainstream culture. For Trump and his low information followers, Mexican and other Latinos are not white and their color threatens the racial self-esteem and hubris.

Image 14: Racial Resentment and Trump

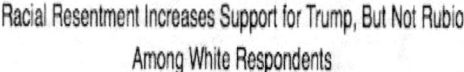

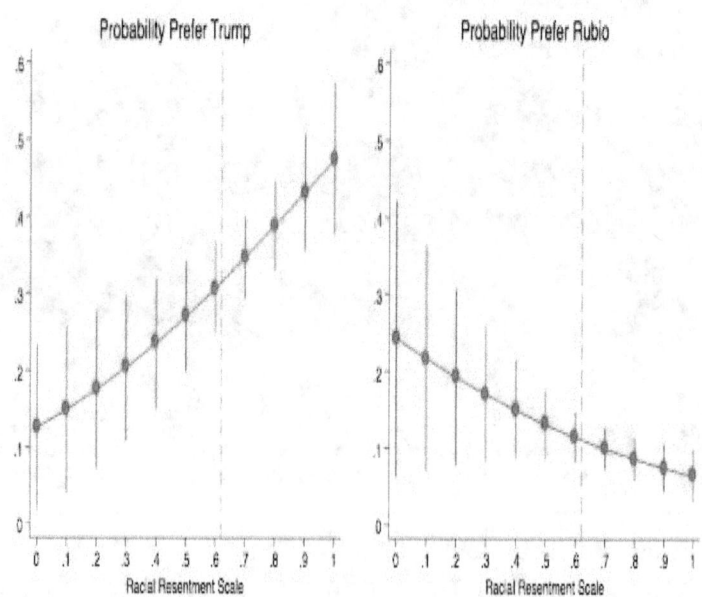

Source: www.thewpsa.wordpress.com

Trump and 60 percent of his supporters have placed a great deal of importance on having a white racial identity. They also believe that discrimination against whites is a widespread, serious problem because minorities prefer self-segregated support groups to promote their culture, build their self-esteem and challenge racism. Trump and 60 percent of his supporters see white unemployment which varies from 1 to 3 percent with the least educated suffering the highest rate a widespread problem caused by the preferential employment of minorities with an unemployment rate three to four times there's. These white nationalists call on whites to work together to change laws that they believe are unfair to their superior race. As a result, Trump and his supporters attract and energize white racist like themselves (Ibid).

The nationalists led by Trump draw on a toxic cocktail consisting of white racial resentment, cultural anxiety, hubris and despair. He offers the antidote of "I will make America great again." In his definition of American greatness, Trump uses coded language referring to a time when the white racial hierarchy excluded minorities like Obama (Ibid). Trump's crude bigotry has alienated vast blocs of voters needed by Republicans to "take back the government" as promised (Parker, 2016). Trump's racist appeal may have a silver lining by exposing how pervasive racism is in society and force Americans to discuss the problem and means to resolve or mitigate its impact.

Trump has insulted every other minority, including African-Americans, members of the LGBT community, women, poor folk and the disabled. But his bigotry may advance the national conversation about race in ways that may assist tolerance. Trump's racism is transparent. His campaign and eventual nomination does present a "teachable moment," whereby Americans may have an unprecedented opportunity to reexamine race and racism in our society (Ibid).

Ironically, Trump's candidacy may also do more to advance racial understanding than the election of Barack Obama as the nation's first African-American president. Obama's two-term occupancy of the highest office has increased antipathy towards blacks by whites who believe his race helped him steal the nation's highest office. This disdain and Trump's xenophobic resentment and conspiracy theories make it impossible for many whites to deny the existence of racism in America, including leaders of the Republican party. Yet, many do not realize the depth of continued racism in their own mindset, behavior and in cherished institutions. Trump's campaign forces Americans to see that our nation is rifted with racism and is far from an impartial society in respect to race, color, ethnicity, religion and gender (Ibid).

A "new racism" has arose with the death of Jim Crow in the South by virtue of the triumph of the civil rights laws that made segregation illegal. This "new racism" is built on racial stereotypes that allow whites to justify the persistence of continuing racial oppression on grounds that blacks are lazy or minorities are stealing their tax dollars or opportunities they earned. It posits that blacks have opportunities and need to take advantage of them like other Americans through hard work and persistent effort. Adherents use certain code words accompanying their "new racism" (Ibid).

Once Obama, a black man was elected the commander-in-chief of the military, head of government and head of state, white Americans became engrossed in the new form of racism. In their efforts to "take back America," during the 2014 midterm Republicans sweep into control of the House and Senate, as well as gained a majority of the governors and state legislatures to block or reverse Obama's initiates at all levels. The anxiety, resentment and anger towards the "others" facilitated the "new racism" and created a renewed climate for white-on-black violence. This climate of racial terrorism took the lives of Eric Garner, Tamir Rice, Walter

Scott, Sandra Bland, among others. It motivated Dylann Roof to murder nine black church members praying at Mother Emanuel AME Church. The "new racism" based on resentment over the gains of blacks created a counter narrative, the Black Lives Matter Movement. This movement spread to college campuses and precipitated non-violent protest to remedy systemic racism tolerated in these institutions tied to slavery, pro-slavers and segregationists, as well as racially offensive practices by fraternities and sororities on and off campus.

"Make America Great Again" From Nostalgia to a Political Movement

Trump's brand of nationalism sees America as great back in the 19th and 20th century when Jim Crow segregation reigned and minorities were excluded from mainstream jobs, opportunities and prosperity. Race-specific immigration was both a legal and de facto practice with racial profiling in those days. The need to reinforce this paradigm helped the Ku Klux Klan to revise and peak, March on Washington, DC, in the 1920s and takeover government at all levels including the presidency (Lay, 2015). Warren Harding, Calvin Coolidge and Harry Truman rose to the presidency during Fred Trump, Donald's father, adulthood through their Klan activism. President Harding was sworn in as a Klansman in the White House in a secret ceremony held by the Imperial Wizard. President Coolidge conducted a Klan cross burning on the lawn of the White House after marching with them (See Image 15). President Wilson endorsed the film "Birth of the Nation" that claims the Klan saved the South and white women from savage black rapists (Trent, 2014). Today, during the 4th of July 2016 holiday weekend, Donald Trump, a son of an activist Klansmen, followed in his father's footsteps by tweeting graphs from white supremacist web sites that are anti-Semitic and racist and defended its usage. Fred was an activist Klansman who obviously taught his son the virtues of white supremacy based on racial exclusiveness and demeaning the "other." Donald Trump's father likely echoed Samuel Huntington's argument to an impressionable son that the essence of America's greatness is its identity as a European, Anglo-Protestant and English speaking people (Business, Day, 2004).

Image 15: Coolidge (Suited) Marched with the Klan

Source: www.jacksonianamerica.com

The son of Fred Trump, like Joseph Goebbels (See Image 16), Hitler's minister of propaganda is a master manipulator of the media. A showman, he grasps and exploits the ubiquity of the social media like Goebbels did with the radio in the 30s and 40s. Trump has sold many Americans on the idea that they need a demagogue to right their grievances. On June 21, 2016, Trump is behind Clinton in the polls by a mere seven points for the next presidency. Trump like Goebbels recognizes the explosive potential of mixing fear and ignorance based on scapegoating minorities to foster tyranny or undemocratic outlook (Irving, 2016).

Image 16: One of Donald Trump's, the Son of a Klansman, Role Models

"Making America great again" echoed by Trump is the same rhetoric used by the Klan in 1920s when they emphasized virulent patriotism and restrictive immigration. The Klan then and now focus on militant Protestantism, better government, eugenics, strict immigration quotas on non-whites, Catholics and Jews, as well as other non-WASP faiths, clean politics by purging the "others" going back to the Constitution when American citizenry was narrowly given, stronger law enforcement on non-WASPs and "great allegiance to the flag." The Tea Party movement galvanized this sentiment in its opposition against Obama as head of state. Trump best reflects their sentiment rooted in 1920s Klan revival that argued Americans were supposed to be exclusively white and Protestant. Trump, like the Klan of that era, championed white supremacy through his narcissisms and hubris aimed at keeping the nation white, insulting non-white citizenry and refuting those that will not humble themselves to his whims (Baker, 2016).

The Klan, like the Tea Party, both of which Trump reflects, faced a crisis because the culture was changing around them, and nativism was their reaction. They then and now fear that the nation is in danger because of demographic shifts spawned by immigration, urbanization and migration of black labor from the South to the North. To drum up these fears, they claimed that aliens (immigrants) were attacking white Americans. The Klan supported legislation to restrict immigration to countries with Anglo-Saxon and Scandinavian roots (Ibid). Trump suggests restricting immigration to nations not harboring potential Islamic terrorists. Immigration would be a very subjective, whimsical and unilateral process regardless of the threats the immigrant faced by staying in an unlivable and life threating situation. This would exclude the many immigrants from Africa and the Middle East fleeing terrorism.

Like Trump and his movement, white men and women have traditionally turned to the Klan for reassurance that

America was founded "by" and "for" white people. White Protestants in the eyes of Trump, his movement and the Klan see white Protestants as the creators of America and without their continued dominance the nation would not succeed. To these xenophobic nativists "now and then," "making America great" requires exclusion, intolerance and vitriol towards the "others." This message supporting 100 percent White Anglo-Saxon Protestantism, restricting immigration and segregation is reinforced every time Americans encounter social change and shifting demographics. Unexpectedly, former Klan leaders and white nationalists are encouraging their followers of white supremacy to vote for Trump as president (See Image 17; Ibid).

Image 17: Trump's Loyal Followers

Source: www.countercurrentnews.com

Trump is repeatedly promising to "bring back" things that have been lost. Manufacturing jobs, steel and coal production, waterboarding terrorist and "law and order" in cities head the things Trump promises to bring back. He and his supporters believe that these things will halt America's decline. To halt the influx of nonwhite immigrants, Trump proposes a border wall paid by Mexico, deportation of 11 million undocumented Latino immigrants and temporary ban on Muslim immigration (Brownstein, 2016). In making these proposals, Trump has forged a coalition of disaffected white voters who genuinely believe that America has lost its way and must be made great again (Dionne, 2016).

The Public Religion Research Institute (PRRI) in 2015 identified Trump's constituency. They found 57 percent of white Americans holding the belief that the nation has declined since the 1950s. Fifty percent believe that "discrimination against whites has become as big a problem today as discrimination against blacks. Sixty-six percent of the Republicans sampled believe that "immigrants burden the country." The American value survey found that 56 percent of the Americans surveyed think that the "values of Islam are at odds with American values." Trump has specifically and skillfully exploited these fears and "white racial resentment, particularly among the lower income and information voters without a college education (Ibid).

Trump has capitalized on blaming nonwhites for economic inequality. He promises to bring back the "good Old days" when African-Americans and Latinos were treated as inferiors, made to descend from the sidewalk and walk in the street whenever a white person walked past them. It was a time when those that protested against the Jim Crow status-quo, like Martin Luther King, Jr., and Congressman John Lewis were met with hoses, dogs and chain gangs. The "others" had to accept the greatness of white supremacy or be "trampled under its feet" or as Trump urged be "punched-out."

The Resurgence of Nationalism, Racism and White Resentment in the United States of America, Vol. 1

Chapter 4
Why Trump's Narcissism and Hubris Captured GOP's Leadership

How Well Does Trump Reflect the GOP's Base and Deceptive Leadership

Trump did get more votes in the Republican primary than any other nominee in history. Yet, he won a lower percentage of Republican votes in the primary since Reagan in 1968 (Bump, 2016). He was unacceptable to a large number of Republicans before his sixteen competitors dropped out. As the presumptive nominee for the presidency as of July 5, 2016, Trump has amassed roughly 70 percent of the GOP support for being endorsed the Republican party's nominee for the 2016 presidential election. Romney and a number of GOP leaders have refused to endorse Trump because they find him lacking conservative principles, is a self-serving, narcissist, braggart and brazen con-artist.

Reflecting the Social Darwin "win at all cost" mindset, Trump's politics mirrored the hypocrisy of the leading Republican and conservative politicians. Placing his own interest over the campaign and common good, Trump has spent a record amount of his campaign fund to patronize his own businesses and lifestyle. The majority of the campaign funds, $2 million was spent on Trump's jet that ferried him around on rallies and business deals. Campaign funds were also used for expensive meals, logging, and his own companies to manage payroll and run Trump Tower Commercial LLC (See Image 18). Contrary to being self-funded, Trump has loaned his campaign roughly 54 million during the primary (See Image 19). He is using web donations to repay the creditors that he does not stiff. In sum, millions of dollars are being funneled into his own pockets and that of his followers in his presidential bid (Ibid). It is unsurprising that his campaign has 1/40th the savings of his Democratic opponent. Respectively, one should not be surprised that his campaign is having a difficult time raising funds from the donor-class. Donors are cautious about donating to any candidate that will use their donation to finance their own lifestyle rather than their own special interests. It is in the interest of said donors to donate to campaigns that would give them greater returns through desirable policies or laws rather than fund a master con-artist's ego.

Image 18: Trump Caught Siphoning Off Campaign Funds to Trump Enterprises

recipient	sum
TRUMP TOWER COMMERCIAL LLC	712185.08
TRUMP RESTAURANTS LLC	137690.79
THE TRUMP CORPORATION	128074.70
TRUMP PAYROLL CORP	102352.63
TRUMP PLAZA LLC	99000.00
TRUMP CPS LLC	66000.00
TRUMP NATIONAL GOLF CLUB	35845.00
TRUMP INTERNATIONAL GOLF CLUB, L.C.	29715.42
TRUMP NATIONAL DORAL	25927.19
TRUMP INTERNATIONAL HOTEL AND TOWER CHI	10818.59
TRUMP OLD POST OFFICE LLC	5000.00
ERIC TRUMP WINE MANUFACTURING, LLC	4991.58
TRUMP SOHO	4865.44
TRUMP INTERNATIONAL HOTEL	2876.98
TRUMP INTERNATIONAL HOTEL AND TOWER	1380.54
TRUMP VIRGINIA ACQUISITIONS, LLC	983.68
TRUMP INTL HOTEL	671.18
TRUMP GRILL	607.59
TRUMP HOTEL	573.46
TRUMP ICE LLC	399.73
TRUMP SOHO NEW YORK	100.00
TRUMP CAFE	94.61

Source: www.occupydemocrats.com

**Image 19: Trump Is Paying Himself Off to
Run for President**

Source: www.thedailybeast.com

As of July 5, 2016, Trump has a meager war chest of little more than 1.3 million on hand compared to over $42 million saved by Mrs. Clinton for the 2016 presidential campaign. Trump has funneled cash into his own personal businesses. He has spent boat loads of campaign cash to fly himself and family across the nation and reinvesting funds into his own business ventures. Trump's own actions contradicted the blustered hubris that he is a responsible businessman and good money manager. He has been tearing through his money at a fast pace and not replacing it (Taylor, 2016).

Trump has made all sorts of expensive promises, including major tax cuts for the wealthiest Americans and corporations. He has promised to cut the deficit, significantly grow domestic jobs and economic development by taxing outsourcing and imports. This plan is likely to cause record inflation and make products and services unaffordable. With consumers made more deficient in terms of purchasing power in a Trump scenario, retail employers would go bankrupt like his casinos in Atlantic City and lead to another Great Recession like that of the last Republican supply-side president, George W. Bush. The American middle class would once again lose their footing. The mega-billionaires, like Trump, could once again buy low from all the bankruptcies created and sell high for enormous returns. Vendors, creditors, former employers and taxpayers become the losers.

An aggressive sales pitch that panders to interest without a specific plan does not guarantee constructive results. Trust me may work in an autocracy but this nation has three equal branches of government and three levels (federal, state and local). Republicans that hold a majority are pursuing policies that severely contradict Trump's promises to appeal to the white working class like "free trade" or outsourcing, freeing businesses from federal oversight, minority outreach, tax relief for all, especially businesses, etc. There is a bipartisan inertia against Trump's reckless populism. In response, Trump sees himself running against both parties. He claims that the system is fixed against the working-class while inferring that this group is white and people of color love him because he gets them jobs. Keep in mind, during slavery all blacks were employed but received mere pittance (leftovers from pigs, hand me down clothing and a shack as shelter) for their labor.

Trump's supporters claim he is a successful businessman because of his billions in assets. What is unknown and he refuses to reveal is his tax return that would factor in liabilities, taxes paid, charitable donations and net worth, as well as verify his claims respecting business success. What is verifiable at this point disqualifies him as a transparent nominee, successful as a businessman and public servant. His self-service campaign appears to be nothing but a long scam with no real intention to change the predatory climate that made him and his family so wealthy. He is a product of a paternal lineage, particularly his grandfather, who has extorted, cheated and illicitly stolen from others (Ibid). His grandson has stiffed creditors and vendors alike to reap a fortune. As Marco Rubio said in the primary in regard to Trump's economic decision making, he could have invested his inheritance in the stock market and reap a larger fortune than settle for less from risky ventures.

Many of the product Trump displays are made offshore. Much of his wealth is derived from cheap foreign labor. His enterprises import shirts, eyeglasses, perfumes, cuff links and suits made in Bangladesh, China, Honduras and other low-wage countries (Helderman & Hamburger, 2016). His political party, the Republicans, are champions of outsourcing. It is easy to tell the white working class that he will stop the outsourcing of jobs by withdrawing from treaties, raising import taxes and setting-off trade wars for their vote. But this "win-at-all-cost" mentality is irresponsible if achieved and likely to be obstructed by both parties. The inflation and cheap dollar would bring down the economy. The collapse of the British economy after Trump like conservatives conned voters into approving a Brexit demonstrates the irresponsible consequences of his white nationalist populism, anti-intellectualism and xenophobia.

Trump who is a hypocrite, enriching himself with oversea labor while blasting the practice for political gain is no fool. He is attempting to con low information voters into electing him to the highest office. As mentioned, if he would succeed in his promise to curb imports and exports of low wage jobs, the US economy would likely collapse as the price of goods and services would further exceed consumers buying power. Republicans would once against manufacture a war abroad to distract Americans from the failure of the economy and quality of life while adding another 20 trillion to the deficit under their tenure.

Despite making and continuing to extract a fortune from outsourcing businesses like golf courses, Trump is hypocritically telling Americans that they must stop companies from moving to Mexico and abroad for higher returns. In a global market system, businesses must remain competitive by maximizing profits by decreasing cost. The most expensive cost to businesses is labor. Other cost like machinery and energy are generally fixed. Trump's populist rhetoric is a threat to keeping our businesses competitive and able to product the products demanded by Americans at the lowest cost to consumers. The Republican Party is fully owned by businesses that pay for their campaigns and conventions. In turn, Trump is struggling to secure campaign donations. The Republican convention on 18th of July has lost sponsors. Businesses are unwilling to support a nominee whose rhetoric if applied would destroy their businesses or stunt their growth.

More like an insurgent or revolutionary, Trump blames politicians' dependent on donations for the economic problems facing the working class. Trump sees these career politicians as "forgetting the middle class." This statement like many said by Trump is a series of code words that signal that the "American middle class" is white and Protestant, like him. A decade ago, Trump was an outspoken champion of outsourcing saying that it "creates jobs in the long run" and that it is good for the overall economy. He does argue that the loss of jobs is an unfortunate part of progress (Choma, 2016).

When "the Apple Does Not Fall Far from the Tree"

Trump's scamming Americans with racial fears can easily be traced to a grandfather who was a pimp and tax evader, as well as father who was a member of the Ku Klux Klan (See Image 20). Frederick Trump, the grandfather from Germany, made the family's intergenerational fortune from operating a boom town hotel, restaurant and brothel during the Gold Rush in the Canadian Yukon. Most of the cash extracted came from the sale of liquor and sex. Frederick Trump established a money grubbing legacy. Lies and indecent behavior became the means to an end, treasure or wealth (King, 2015).

Image 20: Donald Trump "Like Father and Grandfather"

Source: www.ahtribune.com

Fred Trump, like his son Donald, was born rich strictly because of the nefarious activities of Frederick Trump. Donald's father became a wealthy real estate magnate in New York City. On June 1927, Fred and 1,000 Klansmen confronted 100 New York City Policemen in queens over racist activities against blacks. He and six others Klansmen were arrested. They were leading efforts to deny decent housing to African-Americans (Ibid).

In 1971, Donald Trump joined his father's real estate company in New York. Two years later, he was embroiled in a civil rights lawsuit over his firm's refusal to rent to blacks. Trump's counterclaim was that he and his father's real estate firm were victims of a nationwide drive to force owners of moderate and luxury apartments to rent to welfare recipients. His reaction and the legacy of like-minded men who walked over the backs of Other Americans to gain and secure wealth falls short of greatness or success professed.

Trump's racism and xenophobia brought him the largest and most loyal base among the sixteen Republican vying for the nomination (Rosenfeld, 2015). He encouraged white violence against non-violent "Black Lives Matter" protesters initially in his rallies (See Image 21). Public outcry curbed this racially provocative behavior. But, the penchant to use violence against nonwhites was exposed beneath the surface of his and other right-wingers political discourse. Trump is their formidable leader because he grants legitimacy to most racist notions held by the GOP's white nationalist base (Follow, 2015).

Image 21: Trump Encouraging Violence Against the 'Other'

Source: www.nytimes.com

The most plainly, explicitly, straightforward racist campaign by Trump now exceeds that of George Wallace in 1968 and Strom Thurmond in 1948. This was done by getting a record number of whites to vote on the basis of racial resentment. Trump did so by adopting a retro racism telling voters in no uncertain terms that if you are looking for a presumptive nominee who will indulge and validate your ugliest impulse, he is the man. The number of his supporters exceed any other Republican candidate for that presumptive nomination (Waldman, 2015). As for the presidency, race-baiting has been at the core of the Republicans' victories since Lee Atwater introduced it to help President Nixon sweep to a second term.

Distinct from predecessors pandering to racial resentment without using explicitly racist language, Trump has dropped this pretense and admitted that his campaign is actually racist against certain nonwhite groups (Ibid; Terkel, 2016). Momentarily, he tells everyone that these nonwhite groups that he insults love him as if they either are ignorant of their own interest or put him ahead of it. Trump's openness on race occurred as a prolonged self-inflicted error that he doubled-down on. Trump called the judge of a Mexican-American lineage born in Indiana a hater, a Mexican and unable to justly try the civil suit against him because he is building a wall. Trump has been demonstrative in voicing his problem with "the Hispanics" in his rallies to the cheers of xenophobic nationalist supporters. He has slightly backed away from some of his blatant Islamophobia, on an interview on CBS's "Face the Nation," Trump acknowledged that he alienated Muslim-Americans voters by calling for a ban on Muslims refugees from entering the United States because a small fraction are terrorists or are radicalized (Ibid). Yet, his references to "Islamic terrorist" massacring innocent Muslims is never mentioned because it does not fit in his "we versus them" Islamophobia paradigm.

Trump's ascendancy was launched through racially based birther suspicions against President Obama, the nation's first African-American to be elected to this highest office. These suspicions are baseless. Last year he tweeted another categorical lie claiming 81 percent of white homicide victims are killed by blacks (Hinkle, 2016). The actual figure is 15 percent. The 81 percent is white-on-white homicides. Blacks actually commit 90 plus percent of the murders of other blacks.

The presumptive nominee of the Republican Party, claimed that Mexican immigrants are drug dealers and rapists. Trump has threated to deport 11 million while building a wall on the border so they could not illegally cross (Ibid). The truth is these immigrants generally evade breaking laws that would draw the attention of authorities, get arrested and deported from jobs they were recruited to do and source of support for their families. Trump's proposal would hold the undocumented Mexicans responsible for atypical sociopath among them and divide families comparable to what slaveholders did with their African-American slaves.

Trump's coarse and racist language is being emulated by young people. Students at a predominantly white school held signs and chanted "Build the wall" at a basketball game against a predominantly Latino school. Third-graders in Fairfax told their immigrant classmates that they will be "sent home." Hate filled messages have been posted in public places attributed to Trump's words. Trump's fans have been caught screaming "Motherf_ _ _ king tacos" at Latinos. In one instance in Wichita, Trump's fans promised to throw Latinos "over the wall" (Ibid).

The favorite of the racist base of the Republican Party, Trump has been endorsed by David Duke, the former Grand Wizard of the Ku Klux Klan and other white nationalists. To these extremists, Trump understands the real sentiment of America. They applaud Trump's proposal to deport illegal immigrants and his statement of the "clear and present danger" of their presence in our nation. Among Trump's endorsers is James Edwards, a man who has warned whites against interracial marriage, called slavery the best thing that ever happened to blacks, and features a roster of like-minded white supremacists on his radio show (Obeidallah, 2015).

Neo-Nazi websites, like the Daily Stormer, posted articles professing that "We are all Donald Trump Now." The list of such white nationalist supporters is exceedingly long. In addition, Trump has not made it clear that he really disavows these hate groups or their followers. To avoid total alienation by the establishment, Trump claims he is unaware of these groups and has not accepted their endorsement (Ibid). Fact checkers have diagnosed that nearly 70 percent of Trump's statements are lies or exaggerations. Unfortunately, too many low-information Americans are buying the con he is selling (See Image 22).

Image 22: Trump's Support Among Low Information Voters

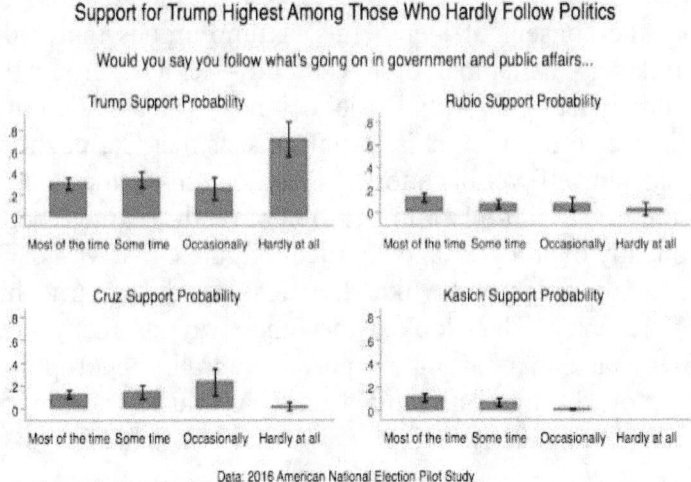

Source: www.thepsa.wordpress.com

A Trump surrogate, Jerry Lord claims that Speaker Ryan's condemnation of Trump's identity politics is racist. Lord accuses Ryan of being racist because he is using the race card against Trump. In the Trump camp, anyone who points out bigotry is a racist rather than individual(s) insulting and discriminating against those of other races like their patron, Trump. Trump also did instruct his surrogates to attack any journalist that questions his racist comments about the judge overseeing the Trump University case as racist. The attack on Ryan was precipitated by the Speaker claiming that Trump was practicing the textbook definition of racism in his characterization of the Mexican-American judge overseeing the civil case against him. Ryan points out that its absolutely unacceptable to claim a person cannot do their job because of their race. Trump, in turn, called the Speaker of the House a racist (Easley, 2016).

In late May, 2016, Trump unleashed a despicable tirade on Judge Curiel – a US citizen born of Mexican immigrants in Indiana – solely because of his heritage. This personal attack is irrelevant to the Republican bid for the presidency and Trump's Party's efforts to "take back the government" from the consent of Democrats. Trump argues that Judge Curiel was a member of a very pro-Mexican group that would object to his wall. Curiel belongs to an association of Latino legal professionals. Trump insists that Curiel should recuse himself, yet his attorneys have not made that request before the court. Trump's problem with Latinos began publically over a year ago yet media figures, like MSNBC's Joe Scarborough and Mika Brzezinski, coddled up to him until recently. They looked the other way, as many other Americans did, as Trump proposed a morally-bankrupt plan to deport 11 million Latinos and bar Muslims from our nation (Ortiz, 2016).

The Resurgence of Nationalism, Racism and White Resentment in the United States of America, Vol. 1

Chapter 5
How Trump's White Nationalism and Hubris Can Lead to the Fall of America

The Thin Line Between Trump's Nationalism and Ethnic Cleansing

With a nonwhite minority that is on the ebb of being a majority as early as mid-2020s, Trump's white nationalists if they succeed in making him president and majority leader of all three branches of government, along with state governments, will make the United States of America the nation either the Apartheid South Africa or Fourth Reich whereby nonwhites will be interned, deported or exterminated. A democracy representing the true majority will not last. Trump's campaign and rhetoric is creating either one of these neo-racist, police state, futures. With segregation as high as it was in Jim Crow America, the United States will likely divide into white homelands with a monopoly of political power to prevent the rising nonwhite majority from ever capturing control of any part of the national government and challenging white supremacy.

Extreme white nationalist groups have gravitated to the Trump campaign and have designs on being involved in the selection of his prospective administration. Among the leading groups is the National Policy Institute (NPI). NPI has a nonprofit think tank dedicated to the heritage, identity, and future of people of European descent in the United States. It's think tank promotes the view that white Americans are increasingly under siege in their own country. Consequently, NPI argues that whites are doomed to be a hated minority as the nonwhite minority grows in number and becomes politically powerful. Trump's candidacy for the presidency and presumptive nomination gives groups like NPI hope for a future that would sustain their vision of national greatness based on a White Protestant Anglo-American identity (Botsford, 2016).

Richard Spencer presides over the NPI. He has expressed an openness to some kind of nonviolent ethnic cleansing that would result in the deportation of illegal immigrants as proposed by Trump. Spencer and Trump also share a dislike of affirmative action for black and Latino people. Spencer and NPI believe that Trump does not share their belief in the separation of races. But, they are strongly in agreement with Trump's tough stance on immigration and non-interventionist foreign policy (Ibid).

Republican leaders, like House Speaker Paul Ryan, are uncomfortable with Trump's xenophobia and racist rhetoric, as well as his white nationalist following. Yet, he and other Republican conservatives have failed to account for their history of power-building by inflaming racial bias and anti-gay bigotry. Ryan feel that his own words rather than deeds separate Trump from the textbook definition of being a racist. He insists that the Republican Party and his leadership "does not prey on people's prejudices" and its nominee "must reject any group or cause that is built on bigotry. Contrary to his own rhetoric, Ryan is endorsing Trump as the Republican nominee. Simultaneously, Trump is electrifying and energizing the white supremacist movement (Montgomery, 2016).

Trump has enabled white nationalists by giving them a national platform and fundraising opportunities. Specifically, Trump's campaign has become "a great tool" for the KKK and "a fundraising engine for the white nationalist media." David Duke is telling his radio listeners that Trump shares their mindset, view and vision. According to Matthew Heimbach, a 24-year-old white nationalist, Trump has opened the floodgates of ethnic cleansing that cannot be restrained irrespective of the outcome of the 2016 elections (Ibid).

Like the United Kingdom that chose to leave the European Union out of fear of nonwhite migrants, the United States is exceeding a white society, in number and culture, in spite of counterclaims made by Trump and other white nationalist that the nation has lost its ethnicity and racial identity. White men unquestionably wield an overwhelming amount of the power, prestige, wealth and socioeconomic status. They comprise 31 percent of the population and 61 percent of the gun owners. White men makeup 65 percent of the elected officials. There are 155 million voting age whites in America. They make up more than enough to secure their own voting majority for decades to come. Trump has a record 65 percent of this voting block supporting his nomination. He is hoping to get an even larger share. This bloc has a disproportionate amount of power, wealth and influence (Johnson, 2015). The least affluent, poorly educated and skilled, white Americans are the largest segment of Trump's supporters.

Realistically, the GOP headed by Trump, the presumptive nominee who is about to lose that descriptor in mid-July, does not need minority votes to win if the well-educated whites see his message as more than unacceptable "rambling bigotry." He does not seem to realize that what worked with a white nationalist base in the primary does not appeal to a more divisive general electorate. Instead, Trump believes he can expand his base of support by including the racist network, Christian fundamentalist and millionaires seeking subsidies. Trump is not alone but has been more aggressive in seeking out the support of the David Duke Republicans among members of the Tea Party than sixteen other primary candidates. The presumptive nominee has exploited a base brought to him by Reagan Republicans and galvanized under the Tea Party banner. Trump has held numerous rallies populated by white supremacists recruiting members, as well as selling hate literature and their bigoted "tunnel vision." Subsequently, Trump's proposals are indistinguishable from the mainstream GOP that uses softer "dog-whistles" code language to build a base among low information, bigoted, white Americans (Ibid).

Whether Hitler or Mussolini Like a Fascist is Xenophobic, Racist and Narcissistic

Trump, like Hitler and Mussolini, rails against the "other," most frequently the Mexicans and Muslims, in doing so, he flouts the rules of civil discourse (the Megyn Kelly menstruation spat) and promises to "make the nation great again" (See Image 23) through the force of his own personality and nativist policies. Besides aggressive policies that breech violation of the tenets of being "war crimes," Trump like these tyrants proposed no program. Trump and his supporters are not bothered by the anti-intellectualism and policy contradictions of his rhetoric and proposals. He has on one hand embodied capitalism and yet promised to crackdown on free trade. Mussolini best reflected Trump's bevy of contradictions by being a socialist unionizer before becoming a fascist union buster (Buric, 2016). Trump does use this tyrant as his role model. He does use Ronald Reagan in this role as once a labor organizer and as president, a union buster.

Unlike either Hitler (See Image 24) or Mussolini, Trump has not taken any lives. If he does not become President of the United States, this probability of taking lives is magnified. Between the two dictators their action led to the deaths of 60 million people. Hitler alone ordered the execution of 12 million people held in forced labor camps (See Image 25). Their examples do predict an outcome based on Trump's rhetoric, appeal to fear and election to the nation's highest office (Ibid).

Trump does embrace fascism. Fascism is by nature anti-political. It is contrary to enlighten beliefs in progress, democracy and human goodness. Trump's brand of fascism fully embraces emotion over reason, action over politics, and violence as a means to an end ("I would like to punch him, protester"). Such instincts as articulated, Trump suggests, bring him and mankind closer to their true inner self. As a true fascist, Trump (See Image 26) has moved the crowd by stoking racial animosity and grievances during the tenure of the nation's first black President. Trump as an existential threat to our democracy should be caste as a reincarnation of Mussolini and Hitler's fascism (See Image 27) that can unite Democrats, Republicans, independents, neo-cons, constitutionalist, etc., (Ibid).

Image 23: Trump Makes America of the Reich Great

Source: www.justplainpolitics.com

78

Image 24: Trump is Like Hitler

Adolf Hitler

- Used racism to rise to power
- Proposed mass deportations
- Promised to make Germany great again
- Anti-Jew Fascist
- Blames Jews for Germany's problems
- Thought Jews should wear special ID's

Donald Trump

- Uses racism to rise to power
- Proposes mass deportations
- Promises to make America great again
- Anti-Muslim Fascist
- Blames Immigrants for America's problems
- Thinks Muslims should wear special ID's

Source: www.hcscaton.com

Image 25: Nazis' Final Solution of the Last White Nationalist and Fascist. Look-out Latinos and Muslims Who Resist President Trump.

Source: www.furtherglory.wordpress.com

Image 26: Trump, a Modern Fascist

Source: www.salon.com

Image 27: Mein Fuhrer Trump

Source: www.thehypertexts.com

Some critics see Trump as being more of a narcissistic bully, a shrewd marketer and amateur politician with authoritarian instincts. They claim Trump is not a fascist because he is not sophisticated enough to have any political ideology (Vaknin, 2016). It is evident that the only thing that Trump believes in is Trump. He exploits specific policies or principles that are functional to him, to be adopted or abandoned depending on his personal interests. There is no "truth" to Trump – there is what helps or hurts him. He will abandon whatever helps today and hurts tomorrow. Trump will say anything herein regardless if it is inconsistent, irresponsible and opportunistic to appease his own ego (Byrnes, 2016).

Trump has demonstrated a narcissistic craving for constant adulation. In turn, much of his rhetoric has been unrestrained and undisciplined. In being guttural, Trump has found a political market for his pitch. It is not clear whether Trump really believes in anything he says. Yet, he believes that whatever he says furthers his goals regardless how shameless and reckless (Ibid).

Demonstrating no core empathy towards "others" and decency in his discourse, Trump displays latent fascistic impulses in his quest to "win at all cost." He appears to be perfectly willing to feed fascist sentiment and conspiracy theories as truth if it serves his interests. The GOP cultivated an audience for Trump from older, low information, conservatives that feel they are threatened by rapid and social change and are more than willing to blame nonwhites for their anxiety. Trump became their hero by emboldening their sentiment in his rhetoric and slogans like "Make America Great Again" referring to a more hegemonic white past (See Image 28; Ibid).

Even though Trump may not be a fascist, like Hitler or Mussolini, he undeniably feeds a fascist undercurrent in American society. Trump may be clueless respecting this dangerous undercurrent he unleashed or worsen, he may not care what he is doing. Trump continues to significantly damages our democracy and the consensus needed to make our institutions respond to the true needs and interests of a majority of our people regardless of race, ethnicity, gender, etc. The Republican Party is as responsible for this undemocratic undercurrent as Trump by pandering to bigotry and conservative absolutism for political hegemony over the governed. Both Trump and GOP have prioritized "winning over ever thing" (Ibid). Both have a recent history, during Obama's tenure, of not honoring the outcome of the 45th president's election in the name of their own racial identity and hegemony. Essentially, both have destabilized government, minimized its functionality and fostered a climate of greater chaos, racial animus and polarization.

Image 28: Trump Exposing Bigotry and Xenophobia to Cat Calls of 'Make America Great' from Low Information Nativist

Source: www.salon.com

Ties to the Racial Purification Crusade

Trump has become the symbolic leader of the racial purification crusade launched by white nationalist, like the American Freedom Party (AFP). The latter group promotes holocaust denial and claims that "diversity equals white genocide," and that Trump is "the great white savior." William D. Johnson, head of AFP was a delegate for Trump from California until it was reported on May 10, 2016, by *Mother Jones* magazine. Trump's camp withdrew Johnson's name. But, Donald Trump, Jr., and his father's camp had earlier established ties with AFP. Trump, Jr., has directly met with James Edwards, co-director of AFP with Johnson. Edwards hosts a radio show that features a wide roster of white supremacists, anti-Semites and other extremists including longtime Klan leader David Duke. The program is devoted to "standing up for the Dispossessed White Majority" (Wilson, 2016).

AFP has been integral in Trump's primary campaign by making robo-calls on his behalf in Iowa, Vermont, New Hampshire and Minnesota. Their message included a warning that "the white race is dying out in America and Europe because we are afraid to be called 'racist'" and urged citizens, "Don't vote for a Cuban. Vote for Donald Trump." They also have broadcast their hate from Trump's rallies. The Trump campaign has granted Edwards and his AFP special VIP press credentials to hold live broadcast (Ibid).

Edwards has expressed the opinion that Southern slavery best benefited blacks over white Americans. The Trump campaign has never disavowed these white nationalist supporters for any part of their rhetoric alienates nonwhites. AFP has been screening candidates for Trump's prospective administration (Ibid). With the apparently close relationship between both camps, AFP will probably influence who Trump's camp will ultimately vet and present to the Senate for confirmation if Trump is elected. This cabinet would parallel President Woodrow Wilson's inner circle that endorsed the view that the Klan saved the South and white women from savage black rapist. Wilson's cabinet imposed the Jim Crow system on all federal jobs and facilities.

AFP is pushing New Jersey Governor Chris Christie, an apologist for Trump, for vice president. Representative Trey Gowdy (R-SC) for attorney general. Trump has promised to prosecute Hillary Clinton, his Democratic rival, for allegedly allowing enemies to hack her e-mail and not protect the four Americans killed in Libya, including the ambassador, by terrorists. Seeking charges, trying and jailing previous administrations is unprecedented in our history and typical of tyrannical Third World nations. In addition, AFP is pushing Jared Taylor as Trump's United Nations ambassador. Taylor is the editor of American Renaissance, a pseudo-intellectual journal that envisions a race war, like Dylann Roof (Ibid). Under Trump, the vision of a progressive, inclusive, democracy would be supplanted by the fall of America as "the gates of hell would swing wide open."

Trump's Isolationist Foreign Policy, Brexit and Its Fallout

Trump and white nationalist throughout Europe prompted by the vast migration of Syrians and Africans from war and terrorism into Europe has demanded closing borders, banning immigrants or deporting them to preserve the white demographic majority and isolating themselves from the multiracial world. Obviously these white nationalists are not "students of history." History teaches us that boundless multiculturalism, racial diversity and international trade and commerce is integral to human progress. In Europe's history, the Crusades marked Europe's access to global trade and commerce that brought them out of feudalism and underdevelopment of the Early Middle Ages and led them to the Renaissance. The Renaissance, the rebirth in classic learning, science and philosophy spawned the Age of Enlightenment and Reason. The Age of Reason led to invention of new technology, like the printing press and in mass production, to led to the Industrial Age and modernization of Western nations with the globes highest standard of living. Trump and his isolationist brew wants to digress towards feudalism that produced greater scarcity among people living in these systems. Feudalism with nationalism will once again encourage continuous warfare and the mass destruction of humanity as we know it.

When, Trump like, Brexit leaders got conservative leader David Cameron to call for a referendum on staying or leaving the European Union (EU), a majority of the voters chose to leave the European Union out of ginned-up fear of a globalism that would allow nonwhite migrants and their cultures to overrun them and destroy their national identity. Once the vote was tallied, the British pound devalued and over 3 trillion dollars was lost in the world market. The United Kingdom's quality of life took a significant dive. A petition was launched with over 3.5 million signatures to recall the results of the Brexit and maintain ties with Europe's global economy (MSNBC, 2016).

The Brexit has stunted job growth in the United Kingdom (UK). Scotland and North Ireland are contemplating whether to leave the UK for EU. UK's pension and medical care system would likely be underfunded and may go bankrupt. Another lesson drawn from Brexit, austerity pushed by conservatives in both the UK and USA elevates the scapegoating of others for these cuts to seniors and jobs sought by those entering the job market for the first time by Trump and white nationalists in both domains. The latter's proposal for isolationism becomes more palatable for white seniors and, low information, young adults. But, it also becomes a solution for international terror, greater instability, scarcity, chaos, misery and motivation for war among European nations and the world.

As the implications of Brexit makes isolationism too costly, Trump and other white nationalists popularity and his poll numbers have plummeted. As their quest for power, influence and hegemony becomes more remote, they are grudgingly pivoting from their instincts. Hopefully, Westerners will fully awaken to all aspects of the con-game sold by the white nationalists who blame inequality among their lot and economic stagnation on nonwhites, diversity, demographic change, multiculturalism and globalism. The "win-at-all-cost" and "winner-take-all" quest for wealth has caused developed nations to be dependent on cheap offshore labor at the expense of working class jobs at home, their purchasing power, quality of life and other rewards of hard work.

The Resurgence of Nationalism, Racism and White Resentment in the United States of America, Vol. 1

Chapter 6
Black Autocratic Rule of Europe as the Root of White Resentment

The Intergenerational Roots of White Resentment

The seeding of intergenerational white resentment towards blacks is spawned by autocratic secular and theological rule of Africoid royals of inbreed Moor lineage who controlled kingdoms, empires (Holy Roman) and the Universal Christian (Roman Catholic) Church. Black Moors established this rule and spread this civilization to Europe by seizing the Iberian Peninsula, Sicily and villages on the coast of Ireland and the North Sea. They became progenitors of a Moorish lineage of nobles and royals throughout Europe and Russia that through inbreeding maintained Africoid features well into the 19th century. These "blue bloods," light-skinned blacks whose blood appeared blue as it flowed through their veins after a millennium and challenges by rising Eurasian bourgeoisie brought about the depopulations of Africa, destruction of its advanced civilization and exploit its natural resources to bring Europe and its Caucasian majority out of the Dark Ages. Motivated by a lust to maintain and expand their wealth, power, influence and privilege, these bi-racial European monarchs inadvertently further unleashed a bourgeoisie or middle class spawned by revived trade, commerce, demand for popular consent and quest to close the inequalities in wealth between the masses and Moorish royals. The push for popular consent quickly became nationalistic and xenophobic against the autocratic Africoid royals.

The first step in the rise of the bourgeoisie and governance by popular consent was to demand an end to the Moorish monarch's hereditary and their procured hold on the hierarchy of the Roman Catholic Church. These reformers were labelled as heretics and sought by the Holy Roman emperors and other Moorish Catholic monarchs for torture, coerced confession as wards of the anti-Christ and executed. Nobles protected some of these church reformers, including Martin Luther, from the consequences of his alleged heresy. They were able to form their own denomination under that protection and translate the bible into their native tongue. The actions of these reformers spurred ethnocentrism and nationalism which reinforced "white resentment" against their "blue blood is black" rulers. The Moorish Holy Roman emperors lead a crusade to restore the absolute rule of both the church and their own monarchies. Massive resistance produced the Hundred Year Wars, Thirty Year Wars and a struggle for a constitutionally-restricted monarchy which broke the absolute rule of the Africoid nobles.

This interpretation of history debunks white supremacy. It does make a case for why there is a deep and persistent hatred of blacks by Europeans and particularly by Americans in a nation made up by white refugee of the Moorish rule that lasted into the 19th century. Intergenerational hatred exhibited by these descendants of refugees from tyranny and poverty in the Old World imposed on them by black royals turned their animus into one of the harshest and inhuman slavery and post-slavery mistreatment in the history of the world. Ironically, in the 21st century, "blue bloods" and other admixtures are rising again to lead the New World Order. Race is becoming irrelevant as a determinant of superiority to explain hegemony over other groups of people. Racism is then an excuse for economic and psychological exploitation of people of Africoid or other features for those perceived as Caucasian. It does have intergenerational roots based on "white resentment" drawn from tyranny imposed by Africoid rulers upon Europe's underclass under these monarchs. The evidence gathered and interpreted respecting this research strongly suggest that power, its abuse, hegemony, greed, hubris, deprivation and rebellion are not the exclusive domain of any particular racial group that has experienced the rise and fall of its civilization. Pursuit of the truth frees the seeker from preconceived biases "by" and "for" the ruling class.

Black Autocratic Rule of Europe, 700-1848

Blacks and progenitors ruled Europe as royals, nobles and clergymen from the fall of the Roman Empire in 500 to 1848 when parliamentary government abridge the authority of the royals. Their hereditary authority prevailed through the period of African enslavement into the colonization of Africa. During the enslavement period, royals personally hide their Africoid/Moorish features with white powders or egg shell mix to lighten their skin and wigs to cover their wooly or nappy hair. Regardless, their Africoid features were captured in contemporary drawing, paintings and other imagery. During the 19th century, nationalism made European rule by Black Moors and Ottoman Turks unacceptable and as a motive for the many popular revolutions for parliamentary governance reflective of the white ethnic group being govern. During that same century, scientific racism was invented to justify each white ethnic groups alleged higher hierarchical status over so-called lesser ethnicities and races, like the blacks. Images of the European royals were quickly whitened to fit the ethnocentric perception of the govern. Xenophobia and resentment for the long-held Moorish rule cause the massive suppression of the "others" contribution to civilization, as well as their true role in the history of the world. To acquire the truth, researchers must rely on contemporary sources and images closest to events and weed-out ethnocentrically falsified images and suppressed accounts of what happens and the role players.

By weeding-out the falsified images and suppressed accounts, the underling motive for the Protestant Reformation becomes breaking the absolute rule of the

Moorish rule endorsed by the Catholic Church controlled by the black rulers' family members (See Image 29) for their own lust for power, esteem, and wealth. True accounts and messages of Christ were either destroyed or censored. Parishioners were prohibited from independently and directly reading and interpreting the scripts. In addition, bibles were written in Latin rather than a common Indo-European language. The education to read Latin scripts was unavailable to most commoners.

**Image 29: Inbreed Black Moorish Hegemony
Over the Catholic Church**

Saint Catherine of Siena before the Pope at Avignon (Pope Gregory XI), by Giovanni di Paolo (1460)
Sources: www.realhistoryww.com

Martin Luther, the cleric who lead the Protestant Reformation, argued for greater accountability respecting how Christians are ruled by purging the unholy corruption of nobles buying positions in the church's hierarchy and repentances. By promoting self-determination in respects to reading, interpreting, researching, and translating Christian scriptures, Luther opened the door of inquiry into other intellectual pursuits censored or banned by the Roman Catholic Church. In effect, he and his movement broke the taboo against using Islamic accounts, often written in Greek, of the Kemet/Nubia hegemony in the ancient world over all knowledge, civilization and religion. In order to fully interpret scriptures, researchers had to rewrite the bible from its Greek and Hebrew sources. In doing so, they needed the Islamic accounts of the context of the ancient world which it was written.

Martin Luther is described by contemporaries as "swarthy" which meant ones' complexion was black or brown, typical of people of Black African lineage. The "swarthy" description was used from the beginning of the Christian era to the height of the African Transatlantic Slave Trade in the 17th to 18th century to describe black people. Blacks prior to the Christian era where perceived as Ethiopians or Egyptians. Royals, like Holy Roman Emperor Henry III, were described as having a "swarthy" complexion, a contemporary descriptor for black. This emperor was also known as Enrique III Negro de Alemania and Henry the Black (Le Noir). Numerous Holy Roman Emperors were similarly described. The word "Negro" was created to describe a person living near the Niger river that flows through the heart of Africa. Popes were also described as "swarthy" and having Africoid or Negroid features. For instance, Pope Urban VI was described as "swarthy." Rulers of the secular realm, like Ludovico Sforza, was described as "swarthy" and known as a Moor (Jaide, 2015a). Moors were perceived as black or "swarthy." Blacks or "swarthy" persons were perceived as Moors, regardless whether they were born in Europe or Africa. His harsh leadership typical of many Moorish Europeans not connected to identity and needs of the governed, encouraged the French Church to rebel. On September 20, 1378, they chose French Cardinal Robert of Geneva as Antipope Clement VII. This partition of the papacy created the Western Schism that became a problem for decades to come (Jaide, 2015b).

Black Russian rulers, like Vladimir the Great (See Image 30), held hegemony over his people, and those of Albania, Georgia and Abhkazia. The original ruler of Kiev were black people. They became members of the Muurish Orthodox Church under Vladimir. These Christians followed worshipped a Black Christ and his mother as the Pope does today (See Image 31). Overtime, these Moors intermarried with the larger Slavic population that they ruled and assimilated into that bloodline (Jaide, 2013).

Image 30: Vladimir, The Black King of Kiev (980-1015)

Source: www.africaresource.com

Image 31: Traditionally the Universal Church of Christ (Roman Catholic Church) Bows Before a Black Madonna and Christ

All knowledgeable Blacks must have mused at one time or another: i.e. Church leaders must surely know that the Hebrews were Black people, thus Jesus was Black, so how can they in good conscience allow them to be depicted as Whites? The reasons for that are of course complicated and racist, but here is how the Popes deal with it in private.

German Pope Benedict XVI, and Italian (by way of Argentina), Pope Francis I, pray to the Black Madonna in a Vatican Chapel (2013).

Sources: www.realhistoryww.com

Vladimir settled a marital agreement with Emperor Basil II for his sister, Empress Anna, by accepting Christianity for himself and his people. He also sent 6,000 soldiers to the defense of the Byzantine empire to save its form its enemies (al-Athir, 2008). Vladimir is celebrated as a Russian saint by both the Roman Catholic and Eastern Orthodox churches (Encyclopedia Britttania, 2016).

The proliferation of black or mixed raced emperors in the Eastern Holy Roman Empire appointed after the East-West Schism is apparent. Latin historian William of Tyre describes Byzantine emperor John II Komnenos (1118-1143) as having a complexion so dark he was known as "the Moor." Many Russia rulers were described as having a "swarthy" complexion like Tsar Fedor and Peter the Great (See Images 32-33). John II Komnenos appears to be part of a black imperial succession. His successor, Emperor Manuel I Comnenus (1118-1180) was also described as black and Moorish (See Image 34). He ruled during a turning point in the history of Byzantium and the Mediterranean (Jaide, 2015a).

Image 32: Tsar Fedor, The Black King of Kiev Russia (1557-1598)

Source: www.africaresource.com

Image 33: Peter the Great of Russia, 1715

Tsar Peter I, the Great of Russia. painted circa 1715
Source: www.africaresource.com

Image 34: Emperor Manuel I Comnenus of Byzantine Empire (1118-1180)

Source: www.africaresource.com

Underlining the inbreeding among royals with Moorish lineage is the Asiatic black lineage of nobles from Hungary. Black Hungarians were a dominant community in Carpathian Basin where modern Hungary and Slovakia exist in southeastern Europe. Black Hungarians were a recognizable group until they were absorbed and assimilated into the overwhelming Slavic and German majority. Besides predating the Roman Empire as members of the Black Grimaldis, many Black Hungarians descended from Asiatic blacks who were both pure and mixed in complexion from the invasions of Attila the Hun (See Image 35) and Genghis Khan. Black Hungarians assumed leadership as royals who served as proxies for the Asiatic invaders and Moorish rulers of West and East Europe.

Image 35: One of Attila the Hun's Black Asiatic Generals

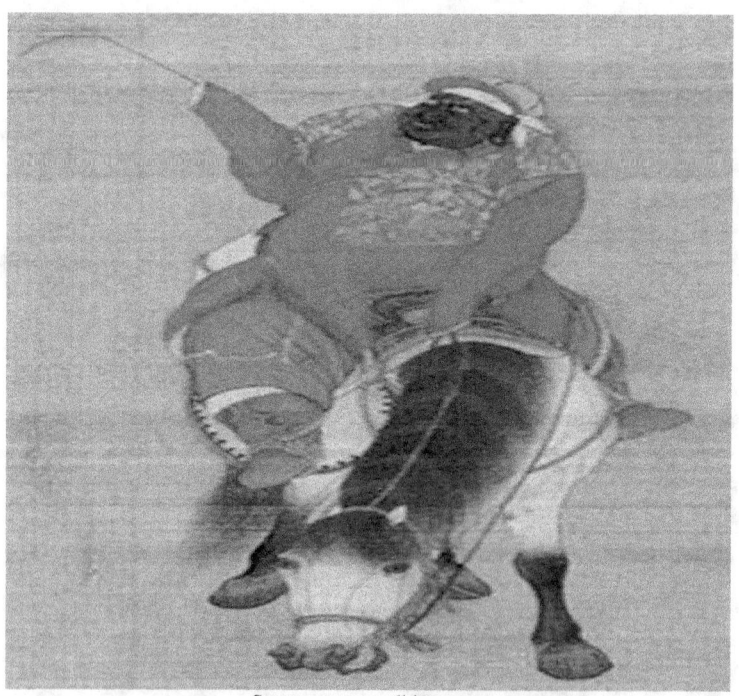

Source: www.realhistoryww.com

Stephen I, the first king of Hungary (See Image 36), established the kingdom by bring together Black Huns, Avars, Slavs and Germans between 997 and 1000 in the Carpathian Basin. By 1288, Charles I (See Image 37) incorporated Croatia into the Hungarian dynastic kingdom. He formed a mutual defense union with Poland and Bohemia (Ibid). Stephen I was canonized as a saint in 1083 by both the Roman Catholic Church and Eastern Orthodox Church. His mummified right hand has become a sacred relic (Engels, 2001).

Image 36: King Stephen of Hungary

Source: www.wikimedia.org/FileSt_Stephens_on_the_throne

Image 37: Hungarian King Charles I

Hungarian King, possibly Charles I (1288-1342) holding the globus cruciger "cross-bearing orb" It symbolizes Christ's (the cross) dominion over the world (the orb). Charles Robert was the first King of Hungary and Croatia (1308-42) of the House of Anjou. From the Képes Krónika (Chronicon Pictum) The illustrated chronicle of the Kingdom of Hungary from the 14th century.

Source: www.realhistoryww.com

To maintain unity and the hegemony of the Moorish nobility in both the monarchy and church, interbreed royals Pope Urban II and the Eastern Holy Roman Emperor launched the first crusades. They attempted to rescue the Holy Land from the white Turkish infidels. Pope Urban II claimed that Christians were being harassed, attacked and banned from churches and holy places. He argued that these infidels were defiling these places. Urban II points out that the Holy Sepulcher was turned into a mosque (Ibid).

The unexpected consequence of the series of religious wars in the Holy Lands was that the Crusaders brought back, translated, interpreted and learned about knowledge banned and censored by Europe's ruling class that would change their world view. They were exposed to many cultures and acquired an international appetite respecting foods and spices, deodorants, perfumes, colognes, alcoholic beverages, garbs, etc., that could only be fulfilled by reopening trade routes. They would have to learn how to advance their art of warfare to protect that trade. These innovations would lead to the exploration of new lands, importation of raw materials and the trade and commerce to facilitate the Renaissance, Age of Enlightenment, Industrial Age, global hegemony and advanced modern civilization. To do so, it became necessary to challenge and break the orthodoxy imposed by the absolute rule of the Moorish monarchy and church spurring the Protestant Reformation, Hundred Years and Thirty Years' War that seriously depopulated the labor force on the continent. To afford these expensive cost, European nations faced the dilemma of raising taxes at exorbitant rates and incurring the wrath of taxpayers who were demanding a parliamentary government with a limited monarchy which could not make such demands without the consent of the citizenry. To so otherwise, the Moorish monarchs faced a growing nationalistic insurgency to ouster them like they did with the Roman Catholic Church.

Challenges to Black European Rule Heightens the Independence Movement's Demand for Constitutional Government and the Demise of the Monarchy

The interbreed Black European royals ranged from half black (mulatto) to one-sixteenth black (hexadecaroon). Some were a quarter Africoid (quadroon) and others one-eighth Africoid (octoroon). They called themselves "blue bloods" because their veins appeared to carry "blue blood" in light skinned blacks who descend from white Europeans by at least fifty percent or more. Inbreeding among the royals reinforced and intensified their admixture trait among Europe's royal families. Off the coast of France, that trait was apparent in Charlotte, Queen of England, Wife of George III, grandmother of Queen Victoria and great-grandmother of reigning Queen Elizabeth II (See Image 38). Her blackness derived from lineage in Portugal established by Black African/Moor progenitors that ruled this republic for 800 years during the Middle Ages. Charlotte, England's First Black Queen, was the bi-racial Princess of Mecklenburg-Strelitz, a German state. She descended from an African branch of Portuguese Royal House of Margarita de Castro y Sousa. Queen Charlotte had thirteen children that survived to adulthood for her marriage to George III (African-American Registry, 2016). He forced to concede to the struggle for the independence of 13 American colonies by the colonist and their French allies.

Queen Charlotte was quite concerned about the American Revolution (Ibid). There is evidence that the entire Moorish royalty was cognizant of attempts to overturn their rule wherever possible, either in the colonies or on the European continent. They realized that the growing white nationalism permeated the demand for a government "by" and "for" the people and they were the target for the revolution to overthrow their African rule and hegemony. In turn, the Moorish royalty hide their Africoid appearance behind "egg shell" make-up and wigs. The growing bourgeoisie found this effort exceedingly superficial convention of the nobility.

Image 38: Queen Victoria (Lt) the Granddaughter of Queen Charlotte of Black Moor Lineage and Queen Elizabeth II her Great-Great-Granddaughter (Rt)

Source: www.people.com

Irrespective of attempts to hide her blackness, like other Moorish royals, Queen Charlotte's Africoid features were evident (See Image 39). Over a dozen quotes by contemporary observers pointed out Charlotte apparent Africoid features. Baron Stockman, her own physician, described Queen Charlotte of having "… a true mulatto face" (de Valdes, 2009). If this observation is accurate, Queen Victoria who reigned over the United Kingdom at its peak of global hegemony was a quadroon and Queen Elizabeth II of today's British hegemony is hexadecaroon. White supremacy is a farcical explanation or cosmetic fabrication for who is capable of holding wealth and privilege in advancing societies.

Image 39: Charlotte, Wife of George III, Queen of England & Hanover

Queen Charlotte Sophia by Allan Ramsay circa 1784.
Collection: Oxford College Anon II, University of Oxford
Source: www.realhistoryww.com

Strong evidence has been mounted to confirm that other noted European royals were black. Much of the evidence has been collected that King Charles II, among others, displayed Africoid features. King Charles black lineage came from his grandparents. He was nicknamed "Black Boy" because of his Africoid features and "swarthy" complexion (ABS, 2015).

Queen Phillips and King Edward III had a son nicknamed "the Black Prince" due to his "swarthy" complexion and Africoid features. Queen Phillipa was the daughter of the Count of Hainault, an area once ruled by the Moors. She was described as "brown of skin all over," like her father with Africoid features. Her son, the Black Prince, wore black armor into battle that symbolized the color Moors wore (Ibid; Hundred Great Britons, 2016).

Sigismund, son of the Africoid Holy Roman Emperor Charles IV, who ruled over the empire from 1433 to 1437, reigned as the King of Germany, Bohemia, Hungary and Croatia as early as 1389. He ended the Great Western Schism in 1414 to restore a single pope to Rome. As Holy Roman Emperor, Sigismund brought together the Council of Constance to achieve this reunification. He was unsuccessfully preoccupied with the followers of Jan Hus that freed 90 percent of the Czech inhabitants from Catholicism. A war with the Hussites occurred after Emperor Sigismund ordered the execution of Jan Hus, a Czech priest and reformer who was described as having a "swarthy" complexion and other Africoid features. "Blue blood" rulers feared that blacks not in their family tree where out to displace them and become progenitors of their own family tree of European rulers. Among this lot of bourgeoisie blacks that best represented the needs and demands of the white underclass, John Wycliffe, another church reformer stood out as Moorish as Hus and Sigismund. His teachings drew a large following of anticleric and bible-centered reformers known as the Lollard movement in England (Real History, 2016). The Moorish royals, like Sigismund (considered "blue bloods") felt that if the underclass could free themselves of Roman Catholicism they could overturn their rule.

Other royals were described by contemporaries of having distinct African features. Dorothea of Denmark, the Duchess of Prussia (1520-1580) was among these royals (See Image 40). Her mother was Isabella of Burgundy, sister of the Holy Roman Emperor Charles V who displayed Africoid features (See Image 41). An authentic painting portrays Charles V as a black man (Annu, 2012). Princess Dorothea looked distinctly more Africoid than her uncle.

Unquestionably the Moorish strain reinforced by inbreeding among royals was evident. To adversaries who resented their rule, their Africoid features were despised. This may have helped to seed or root a black hatred among whites with resentment against their rule a factor in the intergenerational racism that arose and prevails in the West to this day.

Image 40: Dorothea of Denmark, Black Duchess of Prussia (Close-up)

Source: http://www.africaresource.com

Image 41: Charles V, Another Black Holy Roman Emperor (1500-1558)

Holy Roman Emperor Charles V - (1500–1558)

Source: www.realhistoryww.com

Bartolome Carranza (1503-1576) was another cleric described as black. In 1557, he became the Archbishop of Toledo and Primate of Spain. Carranza prevailed in his duties under Africoid Holy Roman Emperor Charles V. He had entered the Dominican Order in 1520. Carranza was a luminary among the elite class of Moors that ruled Europe after the Moorish empire in Iberia fell to Christians in 1492. As a black European Christian cleric, he was called a moor (Annu, 2015).

The Reign of the Black Habsburgs

In 1438, another "blue blood is black blood" family emerged, the House of Habsburg that acquired the Holy Roman Empire from the House of Luxemburg. The cost of reigning in the white rebelling inhabitants under the Luxemburg rule was bankrupting this family. The House of Luxemburg, like many other "blue blood" Moorish families, expenses exceed income from wars to suppress white insurgents that they went into debt to Jewish bankers who migrated to the Netherlands as a result of the Reconquista and Inquisition in Spain and Portugal. The only way they could stay in their Iberian homeland is to convert to Catholicism that prohibited usury that is essential to capitalism, the accumulation of wealth, essential to national development and a higher standard of living. In the Netherlands, they made loans to Moorish rulers to fiancé their wars and ships to explore and trade and resources abroad, while protecting gold, silver and precious ore extracted (Real History, 2016). Dutch owned ships finance by Jewish usury were essential carriers of African slaves to the New World to extract sugar cane for alcoholic beverages and other agricultural products in demand throughout Europe (Wecker, 2016).

The House of Habsburg was able to bail the House of Luxemburg out of its debt to such growing banking interest in Amsterdam. Prior to the Protestant Reformation that would be unleashed 100 years after the Habsburg acquisition, all Roman Catholics were forbidden to practice usury, loaning money for a profit/interest. This canon helped the Netherland Jews monopolize this enterprise and offer insurance for investments and other matters for lucrative returns. With this matter settled with the House of Luxemburg, the House of Habsburg's German King Frederick IV was crowned Holy Roman Emperor Frederick III by Pope Nicholas V. He soon married Infanta Eleanor, daughter of King Edward of Portugal, formerly an African Republic on European soil. Empress Eleanor was 19 years Frederick's junior. Their marriage helped him to alleviate his debts and solidify his hold on the throne (Real History, 2016).

In 1486 the Moorish House of Habsburg's imperial succession passed on to Maximillian I. He succeeded his father Frederick III, the Holy Roman Emperor. His mother, Eleanor of Portugal, passed on her strong black genes to her son. In turn, Emperor Maximillian I did the same for his son, Philip I (1478-1506) with his wife, Mary of Burgundy. Philip I (See Image 42) inherited the Holy Roman empire encompassing German states, Castile from his wife, Burgundian Netherlands and Argon. Moorish Philip's Holy Roman Empire spanned from northern to southeastern Europe (Ibid).

The Holy Roman emperors of Moorish lineage viewed the Roman Catholic church as the legitimizing agent for their rule (Ibid). Popular calls for greater independence and freedom from the tyranny of the church and state ruled by interbreed blacks accelerated. Growing number of whites from the middle and working class became convinced that black gain came at the expense of white pain and its continuation is intolerable. In contrast, the monarchs and elite clergy who were direct descendants of black progenitors responded with stricter sanctions and the use of Inquisition to torture and execute dissidents to feed resentment and hatred against black rule. This resentment

108

would grow as the conflict escalated into further persecutions, wars and calls for a separation of church and state, as well as the freedom to pursue alternate interpretations of Christianity and worship.

Image 42: Africoid Holy Roman Empire Philip I

Holy Roman Empire - Philip I, Landgrave
(Count) of Hesse (1504-1567)
Source: www.realhistoryww.com

The "blue blood is black blood," Charles V (1500-1558) succeeded as ruler of the Holy Roman empire and reigned from 1519 to 1556 when he abdicated to Ferdinand I, his youngest brother and son Philip II. Charles V ruled over an extensive domain the encompassed Central, Western and Southern Europe, as well as the Spanish empire in the Americas and Asia. He devoted much of his rule to winning the Italian Wars against France that were enormously expensive but militarily successful. Charles V was best known for opposing the Protestant Reformation, the medium to overthrow black rule by white insurgents. He oversaw the Spanish colonization of the Americas, including the conquest of the Aztec Empire.

The mid-1600s became a turning point in the struggle to overturn African hegemony and rule in Europe. The "Thirty Years' War" resulted in the defeat of Black Catholics by the white insurgent underclass. The wars created a climate of hate toward black people that persist in the racial animus still alive today among descendant of Europeans that fled to American to escape the tyranny. A number of whites today deeply resent blacks particularly if they gain authority over them, like President Obama. Most do not live with or associate with blacks. Obviously, blacks in a nation, supposedly based on equal opportunity, are collectively worse off than whites and other nonwhite groups. There has to be a reason for this deep seated hatred. For those who do not have a personal experience of conflict with blacks it is not enough to say bias is taught by family and friends even though it is a factor. The roots of the intergenerational hatred or resentment against blacks, particularly their rule, is linked to why their families fled from a Europe ruled by black despotic rulers. Evidence displayed indicates their forefathers and foremothers fled to America to escape the absolute rule of black royals that used both the church and state control them.

The Thirty Years' War is one of the greatest conflicts in European history. It consisted of a series of declared and undeclared wars which raged on between 1618 and 1648 throughout central Europe. The Habsburgs under Holy Roman Emperors Ferdinand II and Ferdinand III with their Spanish cousin were pitted against the English, Netherlands, France and Sweden. Besides being a covert war against black rule, it was an overt war among Catholics, Lutherans and Calvinists. Christian IV of Denmark led the anti-Habsburg alliance. The Peace of Westphalia ended the war. The Holy Roman Empire lost territorial control over the German states. German states won the right to exercise religious freedom and neutrality from control exercised by the Catholic church. Protestants were allowed to retain lands previously secularized. The German states population was reduced from 25 to 40 percent from these wars for self-determination. The Thirty Years' War marked the first successful effort to depose of the autocratic black rulers and their hegemony over the West (Ibid).

In England, when King James II converted to Catholicism and allied with the French, the Protestant majority represented by the parliament rebelled. A Glorious Revolution incurred and James II was deposed and his Catholic son, James III (See Image 43) was denied the throne. Under a Bill of Rights, Parliamentarians proposed a constitutionally restricted monarchy and found a successor to ratify their new form of governance (Webb, 1995). In this regard, Parliament made Mary, James II Protestant daughter and her Dutch husband, William, joint monarchs (Horwitz, 1977). The white masses demanded a government based on their consent rather the will of a despotic black ruler legitimized as such by the Roman Catholic Church controlled by his cousins ruling the Holy Roman empire, France and Spain. The English, mostly Angles and Saxon members of two German clans align themselves with their Aryan lineage among the Dutch and protestant Germans. As a result of the Protestant triumph, the black Catholic rule of the British Isles were broken as it was among the German states as a result of the Thirty Years' War.

Image 43: King James III (1688-1766), Catholic Claimant to the Throne of England

Believed to be James Francis Edward Stuart (Prince James III of England). Because of similarities in armor, hairstyle and Leopardskin cloak found in a Fake "Whitenized" portrait of Prince James III of England, who was son of deposed King James II of England (James VII of Scotland). As such, James III claimed the English, Scottish and Irish thrones (as James III of England and Ireland and James VIII of Scotland). Upon the death of his father in 1701, he was recognized as king of England, Scotland and Ireland by his cousin Louis XIV of France. Following his death in 1766 he was succeeded by his son Charles Edward Stuart in the Jacobite Succession. Two wars to restore the Stuart's to the kingship of Britain failed, (the Jacobite wars).

Source: www.realhistoryww.com

Moorish royals evidently dominated succession to the throne among the kings and queens of England, Scotland and Ireland from the 15th onward. Efforts to whiten all evidence of their images surged from the enslavement of the Africans in the 17th century and peaked during the era of scientific racism that peaked during the 19th century. Only recently the Brits have admitted to being ruled by Black Moors up until the Modern Era. The admissions identified by Real History.com were barely audible and detectable to the general public.

Some of the most prominent kings and queens were identified and have recently been confirmed as have Moorish black lineage. These significant British royals include James I who hand the bible translated into English for his literate subjects to read; Charles Stuart nicknamed "Black Boy;" and, Anne the last of the Stuarts. James I (1566-1625) ruled Great Britain until his death. He was the first ruler from the House of Stuart. King James succeeded Queen Elizabeth after her death. He became the first British monarch to rule both England and Scotland. James authorized the settlement of Jamestown, the first colony of the thirteen colonies in 1606 which would become states after winning their independence in 1781. The King authorized the Virginia Company of London to plant the foundation of the future United States of America. The enterprise proved to be a moneymaker for the Crown and encourage further settlements (Jaide, 2011). At home, King James I (See Image 44) sponsored the continuation of the "Golden Age" of Elizabethan literature and drama. Under his watch, William Shakespeare, John Donne, Ben Jonson and Sir Francis Bacon thrived as writers. His sponsorship of the translation of the Bible would to this day be named "the Authorized King James Version" (Ibid).

Black King Charles Stuart of England (1630-1685) was the most beloved Stuart ruler. His Africoid features include a full lower lip, dark complexion, black hair and dark brown eyes derived from Moorish de Medici lineage (See Image 45). In addition, opponents identified him as 'a tall black man' that stood out among far shorter Englishmen. His appearance drew the nickname of "Black Boy" that is used todays by English pubs so named honoring the swarthy and dark Charles II (Annu, 2009). Charles descended from the same Moorish lineage that produced William III (See Image 46) who preceded Queen Anne to the throne from 1650 to 1702.

Image 44: King James I of Britannica Who Had the Bible Accurately Translated

James by the grace of God King of England, Scot: land France and Ireland etc

Source: www.africaresource.com

Image 45: Black King Charles Stuart of England, 1630-1685

Source: www.africaresource.com

Image 46: Moorish King William III of Scotland, England and Wales

Source: www.africaresource.com

Queen Anne, (See Image 47) the last ruler from the House of Stuart, succeeded to the throne of England, Scotland and Ireland in 1702 (Real History, 2016). Queen Anne's War was her biggest external challenge, it began the year she was crowned and lasted to 1713. In 1712, an armistice was declared by the warring sides, Britain and France. A final peace was signed at Utrecht in 1713. Britain emerged victorious by gaining Acadia, now known as Nova Scotia. Anna's government gained sovereignty over Newfoundland, the Hudson Bay region and St. Kitts in the Caribbean to control trade. Britain also gained access to the interior to the Mississippi Valley, as well as fishing rights on the shores north of Newfoundland (Prowse, 1886). Afterwards, the British colonies also gained access to the Province of Georgia from Spanish territories, like it did with the Carolinas, with an eye on Florida (Weber, 2009). Slaves were escaping into Florida's swampland and raiding southern plantations for family members and friends with the help of Indian and Black Indian allies.

Blacks rule through the Holy Roman, Eastern Orthodox and Russian imperial succession persisted through the 19th and 20th century. Prominent Africoid rulers included Holy Roman emperor Leopold I (See Image 48) who blocked an invasion by the Ottoman Empire. A successor, Joseph I (1678-1711) reversed many of the authoritative measures that typified Moorish Christian rule and raised the ire of the white underclass for a constitutionally-restricted monarchy. Holy Roman empress Maria Theresa (1717-1780) was also a significant ruler that would be considered black today under the "one drop rule" that was law in southern states in the USA until prohibited by the Civil Rights Act of 1964 and court decisions. She promulgated financial and educational reforms, promoted agricultural development within the empire, while reorganizing Austria's military and strengthening its international standing. Her son, Holy Roman emperor Joseph II (1741-1790) ranked with

Catherine II of Russia and Frederick II of Prussia as one of the most enlightened monarchs. The Holy Roman Emperor Francis II dissolved the empire after losing to Napoleon at the Battle of Austerlitz. Francis headed the Austrian empire until 1835. He largely resisted popular nationalistic and liberal tendencies which he perceived were aimed at overturning Black European royalty (Real History, 2016).

Image 47: Mulatto or Octoroon Queen Anne of England

Anne (1665-1714) was Queen of Great Britain and Ireland from 1702 until her death. She was the daughter of King James II and acceded to the throne after the death of William III in 1702. The Hunterian Museum and Art Gallery, University of Glasgow.

Source: www.realhistoryww.com

Image 48: Leopold I, Mulatto, Octoroon or Quadroon Holy Roman Emperor and Defender of the Roman Church

Sources: www.realhistoryww.com

Codfried's Theory of Black Rule and Hegemony

Egmond Codfried's Theory that "blue blood is black blood" claiming that blacks under the West's "one-drop rule" reigned over Europe as royals through the Middle Ages and the Early Modern Era. He points out that these royals, nobles and bourgeois elites had brown and black complexions and Africoid features in contrast to their white subjects in evidence drawn from paintings, drawings, statues, busts and prints. Codfried believes the evidence is enough to facilitate his own museum dedicated to validating his theory. He believes that proof gathered and his interpretation is pervasively suppressed by a convention invested in white superiority and hegemony from the being of civilization in Ancient Egypt (Codfried, 2011). Kemet meaning the Land of the Blacks was transformed into referring to the color of the soil along the banks of the Nile river rather than the apparent hue of its Black African inhabitants which were re-identified as white like Aryan Arabs or southern Europeans. Codfried's theory shades light upon why the resentment and hatred against blacks is irrationally intense. This irrational wrath is not justified by the enslavement of Africans for their free labor which accrued into enormous wealth and opportunities for whites.

Those who researched the deep-seeded hatred of whites toward blacks wonder whether having held blacks in bondage, reaped enormous wealth from their coerced labor and built a world-class economy and hegemony from them warrants such hatred from their overlords. In addition, a majority of the people of color whose forefathers and foremothers were enslaved, whose parents and self are mired in poverty, devalued and hopeless, are stricken with the Stockholm syndrome whereby they end up identifying with an oppressor more than themselves, family, community and race who systemically and overtly rejects them. As an explanation for this resentment based hatred, Codfried cites Appiah's 1975 findings that European whites were once ruled and despotically oppressed by blacks who brought them civilization and Christianity. These blacks encompassed Europe's nobility who identified themselves as "blue blood" actually descended from Black Moor progenitors reinforced by inbreeding (Ibid).

A group of self-identified "blue bloods" have are reflecting their European cousins among the distinguished, light-skinned, colored population in New Orleans, Louisiana. They brag about their ties to European forefathers who settled in the New World and forged a racially-mixed lineage. They appear to look down upon mixed and more Africoid blacks or browns who have not achieved comparable socioeconomic status from inheritance or professional endeavors. Physically, like their European cousins, display veins close to the surface which appear blue in color, unlike darker blacks and browns. Prior to the Post-Civil Rights Era, these "blue bloods" monopolized elite positions and professions among African-Americans.

Back to the Old World, the European royal families were a 'fixed mulatto race' with brown and black complexions with some looking more African, Asian or white. The underclass white majority were called "Grays" or "Pinks" and looked down upon by these "blue bloods." The ruling Moorish lineage gave them privileges defied the underclass. Most of the white underclass European were illiterate since education was a privilege privy to the black nobility who could afford tutoring and/or admissions to Latin and Greek private academies. The liberal advocates of the Protestant Reformation would demand and eventually achieve publically-funded schools using books in the common language. Yet, commoners were becoming more aware that the civilization and Christianity which thrived in Europe was ruled by black overlords (Ibid). Respectively, the inbreed European royal that ruled the state and church were kneeling down to icons and artifacts of a Black God, Messiah,

Disciples and Saints in shrines inaccessible or remotely located from scrutiny by commoners.

From 1760 onward the notion of human races was created and promoted by white Europeans trying to undermine and overcome the despotic rule of their black overlords. Under their racist and xenophobic perspective, nations were defined by skin color, whites were regarded as superior humans while blacks were portrayed as being at the bottom of the human evolutionary ladder. To justify this perspective that is contrary to Codfried's, images of adorned royals, clergy and faith figures were whitened. Portraying this distortion of the truth as fact falls under the heading of revisionism. It was used to hide an important historical fact, that Europe was ruled by a black identified, nobility and royal elite (Ibid).

Codfried claims that the invention of Scientific Racism's taxonomy of the races was necessary to verify white supremacy. Scientific Racism hide that the French Revolution (1789-1795) represented exploited whites overturning their black overlords. Ironically, that revolution provided an opportunity for Napoleon, a mixed race general, to display the illusion of being a global emperor displacing black rule with his own despotism. Scientific Racism also hide that the Declaration of Human Rights promoted by the rising middle class was in effect demands by whites for equality from their black masters. Racism that whitened fake portraits of black kings and queens is, in effect, a liberation ideology to free whites who were indoctrinated to believe that blacks were superior beings (Ibid). The color line was installed in America to reinforce this ideology resulting from prolonged African hegemony and resentment it entailed over whites.

The authoritarian European nobility and bourgeois elite was brown and black of complexion with some displaying obvious African facial features evident in blacks today. These classical Africoid features included full or large lower lips, snub or flat noses and kinky hair. Racism was invented to get rid of the Africoid rule whether it is more or less apparent. It emerged as a liberation ideology from these "swarthy" royals that ruled whites by the consent of the Roman Catholic Church whose elite clergy were family members and the state they autocratically ruled rather than "by" and "for" the people (white Europeans). Religion and reformation herein masked the racial conflict between the ruling "blue blood" class and masses.

Whites and mixed race bourgeoisie that married outside the Moorish lineage wanted to be free and self-determined. The long-standing denial of this aspiration by Black European nobles have created a deep-seated hatred against nonwhite rule regardless of how benevolent and beneficial it may be to their economic prosperity and standing in the world. These resentful whites included the forefathers and foremothers of those who immigrated to America to escape persecution in a Europe ruled by black nobles controlling both the church and state. The nobility had maintained a protector status that engendered the loyalty of their white subjects by waging unnecessary wars and conflicts. Their popularity was based on quickly winning those wars and disguising the actual cost in lives and revenues to maintain illusion of success as opposed to meeting the actual needs and aspirations of their subjects including self-determination and self-rule.

How Inbreeding Benefited and Led to the Reproductive Malfunction, Sterilization and Extinction of the Moorish Hegemony in Europe

The Moorish royalty of Europe were able to settle disputes without costly wars by inbreeding. In a number of such cases they were able to expand alliances and strengthen their military to wort-off internal and external threats. Inbreed rulers brought unity between neighboring and/or continental nations. As such, they best reinforce the absolute rule enjoyed by the state and church. Rulers were best positioned to suppress the underclass insurgency. Pragmatically, its benefits maintained the Moorish "blue blood is black" lineage and civilization for at least 1,148 years throughout Europe.

One the other hand, inbreeding hampers development. Among monarchs and leaders of the church, it thwarts cultural change and technological progress. Inbreeding produces an ultra-conservative and autocratic ruling class that does not find investment in literacy and pervasive education of the underclass of interest. Their concern is to be idolized as "gods" or worshipped. Displaying this aim, they were more than willing to patronize artists who would construct statutes, artifacts and paintings displaying their so-called divinity. They were either portrayed like biblical icons or viewed in their divine presence. This transformative idolatry was spurred by Renaissance and reinforced by the Reformation led by underclass insurgents attempting to cast-off the rule of the "other." As the so-called blessed, the inbreed Moorish lineage had their "blackness" disguised to hamper calls for their ouster by waves of white self-identity and nationalistic politics in Modern Europe.

Genetically, inbreeding significantly raises one's chance of passing on recessive genes. These genes increase one's chance for mental illness, infertility, heart defects, developmental retardation and neonatal mortality to almost 50 percent. Among the Spanish Habsburgs it led to physical, intellectual, sexual and emotional problems that led to their extinction. The inbreed royal families were also inflicted with hemophilia that led to their inability to maintain the rule and hegemony in Russia and Spain (Lock, Last, & Dunea, 2001). The genetic liabilities inflicted by inbreeding and its magnification of recessive genes made the Moorish rulers incapable of maintain their rule and hegemony over the white insurgent underclass beyond the mid-19th century. The symbolism of inherited titles and ritualistic activities celebrating the majestic past seems to be all that is left of the

European monarchy, with a few exceptions where the state allows them to retain most of their holdings and provides them with an allowance for their upkeep.

**The Resurgence of Nationalism, Racism and White
Resentment in the United States of America, Vol. 1**

Chapter 7
The Intergenerational Roots and Transformation of
White Resentment

The Thief and Transformation of Black Christendom
into a White Manifest Destiny

African Christianity with images of Black Madonna and
Christ dominated the worship of the divine for 1200 years
from Constantine's declaration of it as a state religion until
black rule was compromised by the racial uprising disguised
as the Protestant Nationalist Reformation, Thirty Years' War
and One Hundred Years' War. The Council of Nicaea in 325
AD formalized the process of making Christianity state
religion of the Roman Empire and Rome as the center of the
Western church. Constantinople emerged as the center of the
Eastern Roman Empire in 395 AD. The Western Holy
Roman Empire emerged in 800s about 300 years after Rome
was sacked by the Vandals. The Eastern Holy Roman
Empire continued from the 4th century through the 14th
century when the Ottoman Turks overran the empire.

During the 8th century, the Black Moors gained a
threshold over Spain, Portugal and Sicily. Their knighthood
joined together with Black Muurs lineage among the
Romans to establish kingdoms, nobility and royalty
throughout Europe among the lesser cultivated German
people who migrated into Europe from Central Asia. The
Black Moorish and Muur Knights of Saint Maurice became
the progenitors of Europe's royalty and leaders of the Holy
Roman Church. The "blue bloods are black" lineage among
the Holy Roman Emperors, Empresses, royalty, nobility and
church leaders, both in Rome and Constantinople, persisted
until the Reformation and nationalist wars overthrew these
inbreed black rulers. Popular government based on the

consent of the Eurasian Germanic migrants did not pervasively reign throughout Europe until 1848. The Moorish royalty was either deposed or restricted to ceremonial duties by parliamentary or other constitutional governments.

The Divine Rule of the Moorish European Royalty as the Seed of the Racial Up Rise and Intergenerational White Resentment

The inbreed Moorish lineage controlled the church and state in Europe for in access of 1,000 years. Family members leading the church's hierarchy bestowed on siblings or cousins the divine right of kings or God's mandate. That gave the latter royal and political legitimacy. The King, Emperor or Empress would, in turn, protect the church in its efforts to control the spiritual and secular commitments of the inhabitants. The sovereign would be obligated to protect pilgrims to the Holy Lands and other sacred places, as well as relics to the Savior, disciples and sacraments.

Bestowed with the divine right of kings, the inbreed Moorish royalty of Europe is not subjected to earthly authority, they derive the right to rule directly from the will of God. As so mandated, they are not subjected to the will of the people they rule. Only God can judge an unjust king. Any attempt to depose, dethrone or restrict his or her power runs contrary to the will of God and may constitute a sacrilegious act. When Protestant reformers questioned the corruption in the church and state, these monarchs ordered an Inquisition to pursue these heretics, arrest them, torture them into confessing they are wards of the anti-Christ and executed. These reformers sought protection among rulers irate with this control and continuous wars broke out between Moorish royalties and those that were more Germanic in their lineage until a turning point was established to break the absolute rule of church and state by the descendants of African invaders.

The Thirty Years' War, 1618-1648: The Turning Point in the Rule of Europe from the Inbreed Black African to Germanic and Slavic Lineage

The Thirty Years' War marked the turning point of the numerous wars to remove blacks from Europe rule and end the African hegemony in the West. The series of wars associated with this cause by Germanic descendants of Donald Trump broke out earlier in 1562 and continued into the 1700s against the inbreed Moorish royals, the Holy Roman Empire and Roman Catholic Church held by family members. The turning point, the Thirty Years' War was among the greatest conflicts of early modern European history. It consisted of a series of declared and undeclared wars that raged through central Europe in the 17th century against the religiously controlled Black Moorish establishment. In some ways, this conflict is a replication of the anti-establishment struggle of Donald Trump and white nationalists in the USA and throughout Europe. With weapons now of mass destruction, hopefully none of these nationalist gets to a seat of power with an agenda to use war to reinforce their racial and religious hubris.

Back to the objective lessons of history, the House of Austria: The Moorish Habsburg Holy Roman Emperors Ferdinand II and Ferdinand III with their Spanish cousin Philip IV were lined up against the Danes, Dutch, French and Swedes of Germanic lineage. In effect, it was a racial war over hegemony disguised as a religious conflict between Moorish Catholics and Germanic Lutherans and Calvinists. Christian IV of Denmark emerged as an early military hero until he was defeated by the army of the Catholic League and Bohemians under Wallenstein. Bohemians would turn on Ferdinand II. They were utterly defeated by emperor's forces near Prague (Ibid).

On October 24, 1648, in Westphalia, both sides agreed to peace ending the Thirty Years' War. The Emperor's control over German territorial rulers were reduced to nothing. Germans were given religious freedom and government was rendered neutral on these matters. Lands secularized by the Protestants in 1624 remained so. The Emperor and Moorish Habsburgs were given a free hand to re-impose Catholicism in Bohemia and Austria (Ibid).

The Results of the War

The cost to the German population was devastating in their quest to overthrow inbreed black rule of the church and state. The German states lost almost half of their male population in this war over thirty years. The Czechs lost one-third of their population. Disease and famine played a major role in the population losses. Property was also decimated. Up to 2,000 castles, 18,000 villages and 1,500 towns in Germany were destroyed.

The war spread disease and incurred famine. Epidemic diseases rampaged through the population. The displacement of civilian population into unsanitary and congested cities fueled those epidemics. Typhus, Bubonic plague and dysentery thrived and decimated much of Central Europe's population. But, these loses did end black hegemony's absolute control in Europe. Many other successive wars were mounted to uproot, eradicate or constitutionally limit inbreed African rule. Much of the Africoid population below the inbreed royalty which used wigs and powder to hide their features were either assimilated or purged. The spread of rule by popular consent (people of the purest German lineage) by the French Revolution and Napoleon ended the Holy Roman Empire by 1835 (Ibid). By 1848, the remaining Moorish royals were deposed of their authority by constitutional restrictions and relegated to ceremonial duties. Their image, lineage and most of the evidence linking them to Black Africans was albinized or whitened to look like Eurasian masses that were mostly of Germanic and Slavic descent.

From Slaves and Vassals to Masters and White Supremacists

Societies experience cyclical stages of growth, hegemony, and decay. The "arch of moral universe is long indeed toward justice for a majority of mankind rather than a xenophobic and racist minority that finds albinism ideal. Empires rise and fall often upon the remains of civilizations that proceed them. Masters become slaves and slaves become masters. Blacks have through the Moorish lineage ruled Europe from antiquity to 1848, over 3,000 years. Black Africans from Kemet and Nubia founded Rome and Nubia as colonies nearly 2,000 years before the Christian Era. As Roman emperors and generals, Black Africans ruled East and Western Europe from the 2nd century until it fell in 500. It was replaced by the Holy Roman Empire ruled by emperors and empress seeded by Black Moor progenitors. The Moorish European monarchy pervasively ruled Europe until 1848 and symbolically in certain nations into the 21st century. Including Kemet and Nubia, Black African held hegemony over civilization in excess of 10,000 years before collapsing to nearly 4,000 years of Aryan invasions finally by the 19th century. Europe's fragile and temporal hegemony is dependent on continually suppressing the self-determination of Africans, Asians and other Third World people and reap their resources the basis of their wealth and the highest standard of living on the planet.

Prior to 1492, Africans in the motherland and Africans in Diaspora from the Near East through Asia, Far East, Pacific Rim and Americas were as rich as their natural resources which made the richest people on the people on the planet. The continental divides, nationalities and racial categories, were later written into history by Indo-Europeans invaders as part of the "divide and conquer" strategy against the people of the black lands. As part of their invasion strategy, they intermarried or raped the black women and girls to produce colored or diluted offspring's. They imposed their Indo-European cultural standards and image idolatry as indicators of inherit supremacy over the black aboriginal and diluted offspring's. Both of which were reclassified as inferior races whose labor and resources belonged to these Indo-European vandals.

The end of the 15ᵗʰ century marked when Europeans were able to caste off African hegemony on their soil in Spain. Their continental homeland at this point was controlled by Indo-Europeans in their racial, ethnic, cultural, and economic interest. People of color became marginalized throughout the globe. Europeans who were formerly an impoverished lot turned their destinies around by extracting their wealth from people of Africa and Africans in Diaspora. Arabs of Indo-European descent joined with those of Europe to place greed and profit above the lives of blacks and browns. In return, the largest segment of the world's population was marginalized and left with a legacy of suffering that has yet to end (Anderson, 1994).

Prior to freeing Europe of the African hegemony and claiming the lands of the darker races as their own, the European people were mired in what they referred to as a "Dark Age" of poverty, famine, feudalism, and disease. Their economy would only accept gold in payment for trade purchases due to the steady loss of precious metals to Asian nations. Arab traders realized that Africa's narrow sense of tribalism provided a wedge to exploit Africans. They used Africans' emphasis on tribal origins and culture over any commonality of race and collective destiny to divide and conquer them in nearly every tribe in West and Central Africa. They created a large supple of slaves to feed the growing market in Europe. Europeans quickly realized that these African slave laborers were the key to untold wealth in the colonies of the New World (Ibid).

Before the great displacement of black labor from Africa to Europe's New World colonies, West Africa was known for its flourishing empires, major trading centers and producing some of the world's finest artifacts. Empires like Ghana, Mali, and Songhay arose on the continent from being

Egyptian colonies under Ancient Africa's Global Hegemony. These Medieval empires were admired by Europeans, Moors and Arabian traders who frequented great cities like Gao and Timbuktu. West African cash crop and natural resources, especially processed gold and silver ore, ivory and salt were in high demand (Williams, 1987). These African empires grew to this extent initially as colonies established by Ancient Egypt for trade and markets for their own goods. The streams of Indo-European invasions from Greece and Rome upon Egypt allowed her colonies to develop on their own, in control of their own fate. In turn, they could establish their own colonies in Africa and in the Americas before Columbus to build wealth under their own mercantile system. Evidence clearly points to Mali establishing colonies in Mexico and Ecuador out of trade post established by the Egyptians.

Europe's Temporal Conquest, Devastation, Depopulation and Colonization of African Societies

African societies that held continental and intercontinental hegemony during the Middle Ages, like all civilizations collapsed from various internal and external reasons. Most of all, they became subjected to eventual decline to the nearly 4,000-year onslaught of Aryan or Germanic invaders. The elongated surge by Caucasians that directly culminated into the conquest, devastation and depopulation of Africa took over 400 years from the mid-1400s to the end of the 1800s (Karenga, 1989). By the end of the 19th century, European powers partitioned Africa. At this point, they committed numerous "crimes against humanity" which further depopulated and underdeveloped Africans. Blacks did wage a continuous war of resistance and won many battles against these intrusive Europeans (Ajayi & Eysie, 1970; Rogers, 1972). Queen Nzingha of Angola, Samory Toure, the Zulus, Ethiopians and Ashanta's respectively held off the Portuguese, French, British and

Italians. Separate empires, states, nations and ethnic groups were eventually overwhelmed and colonized.

In the fifteenth century, Europeans learned how to use and monopolize gun powder and armament to kill opponents, arm ships for long distant conquest and unleash capitalism as a system to invest in the military-industrial complex overwhelm African, Asian and aboriginal American and Pacific resistance. Ironically, the long distant ship making was gather from Arabs and Africans they would later conquer. Europeans learn how to make and use gunpowder, an 8th century Chinese invention, from 13th century Mongol invaders. Prior to its use, imprecise long and cross bows were the typical weapon for long-distant combat.

The Protestant Reformation unleashed European nations to pursue capitalism by rejecting the usury restrictions imposed by the Roman Catholic Church. As a result, for the nations that broke their ties with Catholicism, interest-bearing loans were used by non-Jews to purchase advanced weaponry and used to build long-distant ships to expand trade and commerce across the globe, as well as protect them and conquer distant lands. Europeans with guns boarded these ships to take enslaved Africans, gold, silver, copper and anything of value form Africa. The slave trade would depopulate the looted empires and kingdoms of Africa.

With technological advantages in arms and munition, European powers were able to (1) conquer cities, state and empires through the force of arms; (2) dictate political development in Africa; (3) force abandonment of production processes, like iron-smelting, encouraging the loss of technique and scientific inquiry necessary for technological progress; and, (4) deny access to technology despite request from Africans. This monopolization increased Europe's technological advantage while arresting it in Africa (Ibid).

Europe used its economic advantage derived from technological advances to (1) graft African economies into a mercantile system as debtors; (2) disrupt African trade routes and relations; (3) reduce African economies to single product economies; (4) depopulate population via the slave trade; (5) coerce consumption of European goods; and (6) maintain their stranglehold on African consumer markets (Rodney, 1974; Karenga, 1989).

The slave trade further hampered development by prioritizing security concerns in Africa. This trade deprived Africa of her youth, the major source of inventiveness and inquiry, as well as control of their own destinies. A context of insecurity arose as many millions of Africans were kidnapped from their homes, families, villages and societies. Fear hampered productivity. Communities that refused to capture other Africans became targets for the slavers. The demand to capture slaves for the traders further divided African societies (Karenga, 1989).

Christianity, capitalism and racism unified Europeans in their hegemony over the divided Africans. Europeans turned their attention away from killing each other to kill, enslave and exploit Africans. Yet, Europeans failed to synthesize the need and growth of science and technology with the need for human sensitivity and morality or how to humanize nature without denaturalizing and dehumanizing humans (Ibid). They have, in effect, sowed the seeds for their own long-term destruction.

Europeans not only looted and destroyed African empires, kingdoms, villages, cities and towns, as well as enslave and deport millions of inhabitants, they took human souvenirs of their conquest for display in their museums and zoos. They caged Africans in their human zoos to ridicule them for their own entertainment and notions of being the most evolved human species. In their museums, they held tens of thousands of decapitated African heads (See Image 49). Africans were beheaded for resisting their hegemony or purely to terrorize their subjects. The heads were form the bodies of African kings, families, engineers, writers, resistant fighters, spiritual leaders and ordinary men, women and children. The blatant intent of such exhibitions was to prove that Africans are inferior, grotesque and unintelligent savages or subspecies. The beheaded Africans and those held captives in human zoos represented a small number of the estimated 12 million Africans the survived the exportation to the Americas (Koutonin, 2014).

Africans during the "Middle Passage" were treated like cattle. Conditions within the slave ships had slaves crammed together in their own vomit, mucous, urine, feces, illnesses and the stench of human decay. At least an estimated 2 million Africans died during the "Middle Passage" from Africa to the trade markets in the Americas. Another estimated 2 to 4 million died during the march from Africa's interior to the coast. Anywhere from an estimated 4 to 6 million died before being sold in Americas slave markets (Digital History, 2016). In this wake, the "arch of the moral universe …" has made European hegemony "a castle built on sand" on the verge of collapse after a century of dominance.

Black Pain/ White Gain

Towards the end of the 15th century, Europe began recovering from centuries of poverty. This turnabout was precipitated by increasing the exploitation of Africa's mineral wealth and human capital. Millions of continental Africans were being kidnapped and sold into bondage (Ibid). Socioeconomic and political upheavals incurred in Africa that have extended to the present. Roughly, half the human cargo enslaved captured for servitude in the American colonies died of disease or suicide during the "Middle Passage."

African slavery meant a phenomenal gain in wealth for Western Europeans at the expense of the inhabitants of continental Africa. The wealth incurred would finance other explorations into the New World and colonization of Africa, Near East, East and Far East which constituted the Ancient African Global Hegemony. African slavery, the worst in the history of mankind, precipitated the rise of the Western European and American Global Hegemony. The latter achieved maximum return on investments in human bondage and conquest of the land of the people of darker hue.

To achieve the maximum return on their investments, black slaves were reduced to being treated as chattel, property or any other tool to build wealth for generations to come. Slaves were forced to work until they died with an emphasis on maximizing during their most productive years. As they aged beyond their prime years their market value would decrease sharply. This exploitation of human capital to enrich Europeans and their descendants has been referred to as "the worst kind of thievery in the world (Ibid).

Image 49: Belgium Hosted This So-Called Display of the Savage

Source: www.bbc.com

By the late 1800s, the wealth power gap between European nations and African nations had widened so much that European nations no longer feared collective resistance from Africans and subsequently invaded and exploited the continent at their will. Their advanced weapons of death and mayhem were produced by the industrial complex financed by the wealth extracted from the colonization and exploitation of the Ancient African Global Hegemony. By 1885, when rivalry between these European nations threated the continued peace, representatives met in Berlin and arbitrarily drew colonial borders for all of Africa (See Image 50). They had claimed 90 percent of the continent for themselves (Ibid). The wealth accrued was drawn to enrich the European colonial homeland at the expense of Africa and its people. The extraction of wealth accrued from the richest mineral deposits on the globe continues today. In its wake, the people of continental Africa are among the materially most impoverished on the planet.

Ninety percent of the Africans kidnapped by slave traders and survived the "Middle Passage" were shipped to South America and the Caribbean islands their descendants would become America's rising minority/majority in the 21st century. Back between the 17th and 19th centuries, black slaves outnumbered the white Europeans entering the New World. The latter group arrived to reap the benefits created by forced black labor. The source of their wealth, the nearly four million black slaves produced the profits which filled various European treasuries (Ibid). The ensuing white gain/black pain wealth power ratio intensified competition between European nations leading to the world wars that arose in the 20th century. The total wars led to the subsequent fall of continental European civilization that was later resurrected by America's "Marshall Plan." The United States of America (USA), England's former colony, became the salvation and defender of European hegemony, as well as the leading superpower. USA's biggest flaw, like its predecessors throughout history, was the perennial cost of conflicts and wars to preserve its global hegemony and the willingness if its citizens to fix a system that produces widely unequal returns, particularly for its rising minority/ majority (Africans in Diaspora) who are increasingly being called on to "protect and serve" a resentful nation.

Image 50: Colonial Borders That Divide Ethnic Groups

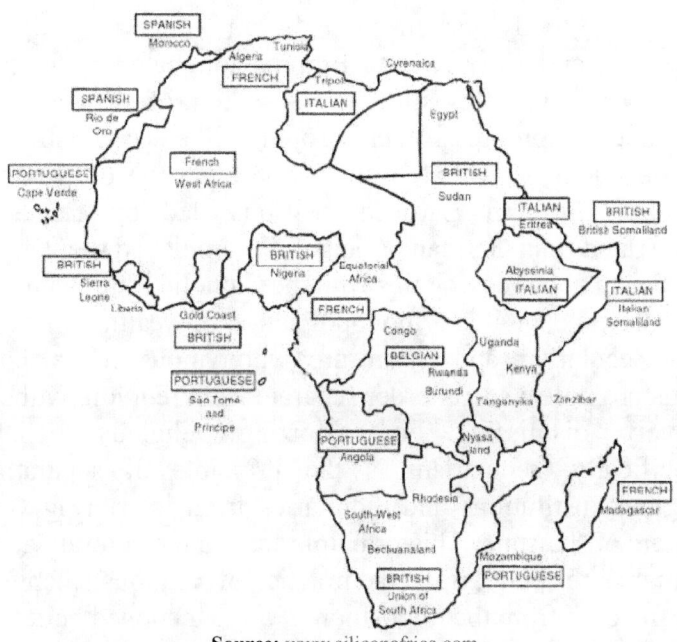

Source: www.siliconafrica.com

The Road to Riches Secured by Access to Trade Routes and the Mercantile Capitalism

The Crusades opened access to new trade markets for European kingdoms united in the effort to free the Holy Lands for Christian occupation, pilgrimages, and worship. Joint kingdom saw avenues to wealth and prosperity through trade in lands formerly held under the African hegemony of antiquity. These lands included all of Africa, Asia, Pacific Rim, and the Americas. The Moorish monopoly to all the trade routes to these lands was broken by the Crusades and aftermath of wars against Moors hold over access to the Mediterrean Sea and trade routes to these foreign lands. Europeans through the ensuing trade were able to acquire greater knowledge of these cultures and its Ancient African hegemonic civilization. To take advantage of this new knowledge, forbidden by the Church as the Mystery System, a new philosophy of secularism and deism was created. The Church in kind used Inquisition to root-up what it considered heresy. A bloody war ensued between Northern European kingdoms and Holy Roman Empire dominated by France and Spain over this influences, selling of offices, and resistance to progressive philosophies like secularism and deism led to the Great Reformation and Age of Reason. Various Northern European nations, led by England, Netherlands and German principalities employed secularism and deism and breaking ties with the Catholic Church and its restrains on capitalism' monopolization of wealth.

Secularism and Deism are synonymous in that both terms promote a social order separate from religion, without actively dismissing or criticizing religious beliefs. Specifically, secularism is the principle of separating religious institutions and dignitaries from interfering with matters of the state. This principle fosters the neutralization on matters of belief upon the practice of religious teachings and freedom from the imposition of any sanctioned belief by the government. Those fostering this principle hold that politics should be free from religious influence (Kosmin & Keysar, 2007).

Secularism is a step toward modernization and away from conventional religious values. In the USA, under its constitution, government is founded by deist with a state secularism that has served to protect religion from government interference and vice versa. But secularism on a social level is less prevalent (Feldman, 2005). As retrenchment escalates in a nation led by an African-

American President elected by a rising minority-majority, the push backwards is led by religious fundamentalist who are trying to prohibit the secularize of government and impose their religious values on a religiously diverse population.

Secular Society provides the following benefits: (1) deep respect for individuals and small groups of which they are members, (2) equality, (3) each person is helped to realize their potential, and (4) it breaks down class and caste barriers. The characteristics of this society include (1) not having a singular view of the universe and man's view in it, (2) is pluralistic, (3) is tolerant, (4) a limited agreement on methods of problem-solving and a common framework of law, and (5) does not have any official images and a common universally applied type of ideal behavior (Mundy, 1963).

The Rise of Excessive Avarice and Runaway Capitalism

Under the canon law of the Catholic Church avarice or greed is a sin. Usury or lending money and charging interest necessary for banking, insurance and investment fell within the definition of avarice and were tightly restricted if not discouraged altogether. Money leading and investment are essential for the accumulation of capital, particularly by the middle class in their quest for greater wealth, income and power. Escalating wealth and income among the middle class dilutes the power and influence of both the nobility and the Church, its ally in the quest for autocratic and arbitrary power and control. From its inception as the state religion of the Roman Empire through Reformation sanctions were applied to those involved in Usury. They would lose grace and even face excommunication or further punishment under the Inquisition in the late Middle Ages.

During the Reformation there were stark challenges to restrictions placed on usury and avarice. The rise of mercantilism since the Renaissance created an economic system in which capital assets are privately owned and items are brought to market for profit. To finance this system usury or financing for exorbitant profit became an essential tool for merchants, entrepreneurs and nations to gain wealth, power, influence and hegemony. Western nations pursing hegemony had to challenge their tie with the Catholic Church to succeed in the new highly-competitive business environment. Reformation became a useful means to cut the tie between the Church and the state while plunging into capitalism and competing for global hegemony. Those nations adhering to the Catholic Church and its sanction against avarice and usury failed to effectively invest in mercantilism, capitalism, colonialism, hegemony and victory in wars to maintain their gains and a favorable balance of trade.

The modern hegemony that arose from the Age of Enlightenment depended on capital accumulation, a favorable balance of trade, entrepreneurship and acquiring cheap or slave labor to produce highly-profitable surpluses at the lowest conceivable cost (Billig, 1995). The economic systems to produce such wealth are called capitalism. Western global hegemony is built on capitalism. Feudalism the former economic system collapsed after the trade routes were reopened as a result of the Crusades and the nationalism this holy war spawned. The Crusades, the war to secure access to the holy lands for Christians was a joint effort by feudal lords and kings with the Catholic Church. Feudal countrymen fought as national units. Once the war was over the joint national and international effort became the bases for diplomatic alliance to secure trade routes from the Moors, Arabs and pirates. Feudal lords demanded greater authority from their kings and eventually the Church. The context for capitalism as the dominant economic system in the Western world was set by the ensuing mercantilists that arouse to pursue a favorable balance of trade and accrue wealth or capital. The capitalism built on mercantilism became the greatest wealth producing system known to man since antiquity.

The Industrial Age, which produced the modern Western hegemony, arouse from the capital investments derived from the Age of Mercantilism. Capitalism and the Industrialism it produces provide the highest standard of living known to mankind in the developed nations. But capitalism bears some acute cost. Taxes had to be raised to protect trade and commerce from intruders and thieves externally and internally. This meant financing a powerful army and navy. Civil law enforcement would have to be improved. Consequently, the lower classes would have to bear the cost of policing these threats to wealth accumulation and safety. In addition, the social welfare would falter as wealth is concentrated in the hands of fewer individuals at the expense of labor and well-being of the many. Governments were forced to intervene in the economy to promote social welfare and law and order.

The collateral damage of capitalism is social inequality, unfair distribution of wealth and power, a tendency toward market monopoly or government by the ruling class, imperialism, counter-revolutionary wars and various forms of cultural and economic exploitation and materialism. In addition, capitalism tends to encourage the repression of labor and trade unions, social alienation, economic inequality, unemployment and economic instability. Alongside the rise of capitalism and nationalism has had parallel growth. Nationalism is a belief or political ideology that involves personal identity with one's nation. It has been a major factor in the downfall of European nations by encouraging nations to subjugate people unlike themselves in order to gain racial hegemony or global supremacy. Germany and her allies followed this path and created two world wars of Western destruction. Since then, the USA that gained superpower status in the ashes of those wars of destruction is also in jeopardy as it has been entwined in continuous wars to maintain its global hegemony at the expense of its financial sustainability. The lesson of the Tower of Babel is that the seeds of the destruction of hegemony are sown in an empires' quest to not only make themselves in the image of God and pursing a manifest destiny but to replace him and force the rest of humanity to bow down to their false idolatry and fabrications of being the exclusively chosen or blessed people on the basis of avarice.

European Nationalism Gave Rise to Its Own Demise

The Middle Ages ended with the beginning of the Renaissance or rebirth of civilization (culture, learning and innovation). The early modern era followed in the 15th century. Nationalism surged after the French Revolution that spurred identity politics; independence from the despotic rule of "others, namely Black Moors and Ottoman Turks; popular rule by consent with codification of individual rights; and, self-determination. The emerging nation-states formed constitutional governments based on the consent of the governed that abolished absolute rule, and created checks and balances between the executive, judicial and legislative branches of government. A bill of rights protecting individuals from governmental tyranny was adopted. These ideas of liberalism regarding "liberty, equality and brotherhood" were adopted. National identity was emphasized along with a romantic view of cultural self-expression through nationhood (Schroeder, 1994).

A strong resentment against non-Germanic rule by Moors and Ottoman Turks continued to grow. The rising agitation lead to numerous wars of independence. By 1848, these revolutions encompassed all of Europe. They resulted in a severe famine, economic crises and mounting popular demands for political change. National struggles led to the rediscovery of native histories and cultures. Unfortunately, nationalism elevated discrimination and xenophobia based on race and ethnicity. Hatred and violence towards the "other" found expression in two global wars over power, hegemony, colonies, access to trade, ethnicity, etc., which nearly erased Western civilization and all its advantages accumulated at the expense of Africa's natural mineral resources and its enslaved and colonized people.

The Resurgence of Nationalism, Racism and White
Resentment in the United States of America, Vol. 1

Chapter 8
The End of Africa's Global Hegemony and the Rise of
European-American Global Hegemony Built on
Slavery, Mercantile Capitalism and Colonialism

The Roots of the Global Wealth Disparity

From antiquity, Africa has been generally recognized as
the richest continent on the earth. God and nature blessed
and enriched its soil. Africa has an abundance of resources
and human spirit. According to biblical and secular records,
Africa is the birthplace of mankind. On this continent,
mankind was fruitful, multiplied and migrated across the
globe to inhabit all continents and habitable islands. Today,
through European and New World capitalism the wealth of
Africa was transported to their banks and treasuries
(Anderson, 1994). The origin and legacy of civilization and
religion was coopted by these invaders. Most of the
inhabitant of Africa were enslaved and transported to the
Americas extract wealth from their enslavers from plantation
labor. Roughly, 50 percent of these transported slaves died
during the Middle Passage from the cruel conditions
imposed, diseases spread by their capturers, and by their own
hands (leaping overboard). For some, suicide is preferred
over further enslavement and being separated from their
homes and families.

Prior to the extraction of wealth and human resources
from Africa, Europe was riddled with poverty, famine,
Feudalism and disease. Stealing the labor and land of the
darker races of Africa, Asia and Americas turned Europe
into the wealthiest continent on earth. Europeans and their
colonial descendants monopolized more than 80 percent of
the world's wealth. The 80 percent, nonwhite, global
population was forced to survive on less than 20 percent of

the planet's wealth. Wealthy Europeans and their descendants claimed that possession by conquest is 9/10th of the law and Manifest Destiny bestowed by God made in their image. This Supreme Being, as they see it, blessed them with the wealth, land, and labor they conquered. The racism they utilized to rationalize their conquest of darker races was rationalized as their responsibility for the "lesser races" along with other creations of God. The lesser races would be deemed as "Servants of the Servants of God." This designation would be inserted into the Holy Bible as the "Curse of Ham." It was removed by the mid-60s when biblical scholars and civil rights activist pointed out that this so-called curse was added to the gospel by pro-slavers and maintained by Jim Crow advocates to justify racial inequality.

Europeans and their colonial descendants have a history of monopolizing and excluding the darker races from equitable access to the wealth they took to maintain their high standard of living. The racial possession of their exclusive access to wealth is justified by a racist ideology which is internalized, hidden from moral discourse, and institutionalized. The ideology stigmatizes the so-called "lesser races" was less capable of using the wealth to advance mankind and civilization because they are allegedly prone to moral ineptitude, thuggery, savagery and brutish behavior. Racism is designed to rationalize the possession of wealth, power, and privilege by the dominant race at the expense of so-called "lesser races." In this society, white gain is at the cost of black pain. The greatest fear of the dominant group is that black gain can only be achieved by white pain and defensively conservatives are stirring-up "white resentment" to ensure the gains of the darker races are minimized or set back.

The United States government founded "by' and "for" the descendants of Europeans was established to maintain preferential treatment through its laws, policies, and programs that gave and preserve wealth, power, and privileged status to white Americans. For 16 plus generations, the government aggressively pursued preferential treatment programs that helped the direct descendants and immigrants of Europe to acquire free or cheap land, black labor, business and employment opportunities, and other forms of government assistance. Simultaneously, government-supported laws and customs were used to deny blacks and other people of color access to the same resources. People of the darker races received inferior education and far fewer access to meaningful labor, trades, and businesses (Bergman, 1969).

Black enslavement would not have been possible without government assistance and laws to apprehend runaway slaves. The government "by" and "for" the slavers removed Southeastern Indians from their ancestral land so that slaveholders could expand their slave empire into the Deep South. The Indians were removed to Oklahoma-Arkansas-Kansas territory set aside for them to become wards of the government. Many died during the forced migration known as "the Trail of Tears." This and other thieves of Indian land, forced confinement, murder, and European-bred diseases reduced the Native American population from an estimated 20 million plus in America to less than 2 million. Without black slave labor to work the land stolen the properties would have little value. Instead, those lands and commerce generated for the nation turned the United States into an economic and military superpower.

Wealth extracted by white families, based on expropriation of black labor and land taken from Native Americans passed on to succeeding generations of whites until the original sources of wealth became hidden by time. After the slaves were emancipated without wealth and the only avenue for income was to work for their former masters or their descendants, the dominant white society increasingly turned away from blacks and toward other means of producing wealth. These alternative means include the acquisition of corporate stocks, public bonds and banking certificates, which were government-regulated and protected (Anderson, 1994). Slightly over 50 percent of the wealthy are so due to intergenerational wealth. The other nearly 50 percent are given access to the wealth on the bases of their connections and race.

African-Americans controlled less than 2 percent of the nation's wealth before the drastic losses in home ownership during the Great Recession of 2008. Their wealth was tied up primarily in their homes, automobiles, and garbs. African-Americans have little wealth to pass on to their children. Few blacks have businesses to pass on. They have been preyed upon by discriminatory policies inflicted on them by the banking industry, insurance industry and mortgage companies. As a result, the economic progress and acquisition of wealth of blacks was impeded. Many blacks were forced into apartment renting or public housing because of their marginal incomes. Consequently, they were deprived of the opportunity to build tax shelters or equity for future generations to inherit. Black heirs are more likely to inherit unpaid debt and poverty (Ibid).

An America Founded "By" and "For"
Indo-European Wealth Acquisition

The United States began as Thirteen British Colonies that fought for and gained their independence in 1781. The British Empire did attempt to invade its former colony in the War of 1812 and burn down the colonists' new capitol, Washington, D.C., but failed to capture the President and Congressional leaders. Britain's failure to recapture its former colony was exemplified by its defeat in the Battle of New Orleans. They did prevent the former colonist from invading Canada and seizing all of their main land American territory. The new nation did expand to the pacific coast by war and purchased of land held by the Spanish.

Slavery helped to build the capital needed to transform the new nation's economy from agrarian to industrial. That wealth was used to literally build a residence for the President of the United States in Washington, D. C., that is standing today (See Image 51). Other federal offices were also built and maintained by slaves. Irrespective of its value to the construction of the nation, the scorn over the immorality of slavery escalated as Northern business leaders became convinced that slavery was an impediment to the immigration of "free labor" from Europe's artisan class that was needed to complete the industrialization process and transformation to a world-class empire. Southerners resisted changes to their way of life, wealth and privilege. In turn, they started the nation's costliest war in terms of causalities, weapons of war and supplies in their effort to succeed from the union. The industrial north and resource-rich west overwhelmed the Confederacy after a long and bloody war.

The South as Generator of the Nation's Wealth

The wealth that transformed a budding nation of subsistent farms and businesses into a commercial-industrial rival to European power was slavery. Slavery was the engine of capital driving the new economy (See Images 52-53). The South's commercial production dependent on slave labor held the greatest concentration of per capita wealth in the nation (See Image 54). The roughly five million slaves served as negotiable instruments or commodities, as well as labor devices for income. Slaves could be bartered or accepted as collateral when currency or other valuables were in short supply. In effect, they constituted as a medium of monetary exchange (Anderson, 1994).

In the South, slave ownership surpassed land ownership as the greatest source of wealth. Any action short of a civil war would not deter a system of profitability and wealth-producing as black slavery. By 1860, the $7 billion capital investment in African slaves exceeded all other business investments in the North, South and the federal budget (Ibid).

Image 51: White House Was Built by Slave Labor, 1792-1800

Source:
https://en.wikipedia.org/wiki/White_House#/media/File:White_House_north_and_south_sides.jpg

Image 52: Brought Here in Cages and Chains

Source: www.nahamet.com

Image 53: Slave Labor as the Foundation of Wealth in America

Source: www.usslave.blogspot.com

Image 54: Slave Labor as the Foundation of Wealth in America

Source: http://www.oncoursesystems.com/images/user/8677/14424/Slaves.jpg
will7083.blogspot.com

Slaves were equivalent to today's credit card. Masters could always earn money by either selling the slave labor or selling the slave. Large Southern plantation owners had 18 times more wealth than a Northern farmer and more than 400 times the wealth of the average Northern urban laborers (See Images 55-56). The slave system had a residual benefit to Southern farmers. Compared to Northern farmers, Southern farmers' wealth disproportionately favored them over their northern counterparts. The non-slave owners were decidedly poorer than those owning slaves (Ibid). A poor Southerner who owned nothing more than two Africans had assets comparable to the average Northerners' personal property, livestock, modest savings and real estate (Fogel & Engerman, 1995, 1974).

Image 55: One of Many Wealthy Plantations Built by Slave Labor

Source: www.victorianswag.blogspot.com

Image 56: One of Many Wealthy Plantations Built by Slave Labor

Source: www.south-carolina-plantations.com

The wealth accrued from the enslavement of Africans benefited numerous businesses in the community and throughout the developing nation. Many Southern entrepreneurs and a number of Northern ones acquired wealth by providing support services and goods to slaveholders. The sales of saddles and other manufactured goods to the South nearly led to New Jersey succeeding from the Union in the Civil War. Some Southern businesses could not survive unless they provided services and goods ranging from household effects and farm tools to the leather slave restraints sold exclusively to planters (Anderson, 1994). While nearly 20 percent of the manufacturing firms serving plantations were located in the South nearly 80 percent of the firms were in the North and imported from abroad at a higher price due to tariffs protecting domestic businesses in the early nation.

Slave produced products helped farms and small town businesses sustain themselves. Massive amounts of capital were generated by businesses supporting plantations. The multiplying effect helped establish and sustain Charleston, Savannah, Norfolk, New Orleans and other major Southern seaports (Ibid).

The Multiplying Effect on Northern States

The Northern economy thrived off the labor of the enslaved Africans by profiteering off businesses connected to the slavery industry. Most Northerners, even going into the Civil War, were not opposed to black slavery. Only a few abolitionists opposed black slavery on moral grounds. Most Northerners enjoyed the fruits of black labor by eating the food, wearing the cotton, and drinking the rum these slaves produced.

In New England where three times as many textile mills existed than the entire South, the mills manufactured, processed, retailed and thrived off slave-produced cotton (Ibid). By 1850, Northern mills processed 25 percent of the slave produced cotton. Northerners were provided with clothes, fabric, jobs, income, wealth, taxes and other benefits from the slave produced cotton. Nearly every Northerner benefited from African slavery (Fogel, 1989; Elliot, 1969).

The business opportunities of many Northern businessmen were tied to slavery predominately in the South. It would be counterproductive for Northerner businessmen benefiting from the products of slave labor to oppose slavery (Bergmann, 1969). Northern shipbuilders amassed fortunes building ships that hauled slaves and durable goods to the Caribbean islands, Europe and other commercial ports around the world (Anderson, 1994).

Shipping industry capital accumulated from the slave trade was invested in the development of major insurance and bonding companies. These companies, in turn, provided policies to cover slave-produced goods transported to market from most ports. Industries invested in marketing slave-produced goods successfully lobbied Northern states into investing in the construction of water canals and railroads needed to speed up the distribution of slave-produced products across the nation ((Ibid).

The North drew much of its economic prosperity from the "peculiar institution." It only pretended that they opposed slavery. When whites in the North faced a Civil War over the succession of slave states from the Union they chose accumulating wealth and power. Under Lincoln's leadership they tried to retain the national economy tied to slavery in the South without freeing the slaves. Lincoln tried to get Southern states that have not succeeded from the Union to force the secessionist to remain in the national political-economy. Only after two years of war and attempts by rebels to invade the North, Lincoln only emancipated the slaves who crossed over to Union lines to undermine the South's ability to wage the war. Without slave-made products, the Confederacy could not cloth its soldiers and exchange cotton for guns and munitions.

The Uniqueness of Slavery in America

Slavery in the United States of America was more profound, endemic and dehumanizing than anywhere else in the Western Hemisphere (See Image 57), including the Caribbean Islands. The sheer number of Africans captured was estimated to be 60 million. Only 15 million survived the voyage to the Americas. Mixed race populations were bred in the Americas to increase the number of slave laborers and sexual concubines. Most of the slaves were emancipated outside the United States. The large numbers of mixed race people and blacks made enslavement more expensive and less manageable. In the South, slavery continued until ending it was necessary to preserve the Union.

Image 57: Slave Labor as the Foundation of Wealth in America

Source: www.understandingrace.org

The skin color of the black slave was made into a badge of degradation, sensationalized and cast as an indicator of permanent inferiority. For security reasons and survivability under inhuman conditions, Africans were chosen after attempts to enslave indentured white servants and Indians failed. Indentured whites could escape by being indistinguishable from the slaveholders. It was hard to domesticate Indians who could and did escape into the wilderness at any opportunity to rejoin their tribes. An ocean stood between the Africans, their homeland and tribes.

Africans were punished for using their own native language and culture that could not be degraded or stigmatized by their slave masters. They were forced to use broken or old English. Learning and reading was first discouraged and later prohibited by law after Nat Turner used the Bible to lead a slave revolt. Under the rubrics of slavery, Africans were psycho-socially conditioned to despise themselves. Self-hatred and racial disunity was both encouraged and rewarded (Ibid). Self-love, empathy and cooperation among slaves faced severe sanctions or punishments.

The "peculiar institution" was unusual in every sense. The word "peculiar" as defined by the Webster Dictionary refers to "something unusual or belonging exclusively to a person or thing." The slavery of Africans in the United States was diametrically different from ancient slavery. It was purely for economic reasons and was the most extensive and harshest known to mankind. In addition, it was purely aimed at black people. Evidently 20 to 35 million blacks were outright killed to bring 15 million from Africa to the plantations in America. They were physically enslaved, psychologically abused, academically impaired and economically impoverished for nearly 400 years (Anderson, 1994).

Black enslavement nullified the basic human rights of the slave. Religion intervened on behalf of the slaveholder, offering biblical justifications for the intergenerational continuation of this wealth producing but immoral practice.

Rivaled and allied governments conspired to manipulate and enslave blacks in order to develop New World holdings and colonize Africa. Capitalism and its vast accumulation of wealth were based on slaveholding. It provided for the acquisition of wealth and socioeconomic mobility for the poorest white person (Ibid).

The enslavement of Africans did not result from war, religious persecution and financial indebtedness. Africans were enslaved because their blackness made them distinguishable from the white population (Ibid). As blacks, they could not hide within a predominantly white population. Their adaptation to the equatorial environment meant they were more effective in the hot and humid climate of the Southern states. In addition, they were farmers in Africa prior to their capture.

The skin color of the black slave was made into a badge of degradation, sensationalized and cast as an indicator of permanent inferiority. For security reasons and survivability under inhuman conditions, Africans were chosen after attempts to enslave indentured white servants and Indians failed. Indentured whites could escape by being indistinguishable from the slaveholders. It was hard to domesticate Indians who could and did escape into the wilderness at any opportunity to rejoin their tribes. An ocean stood between the Africans, their homeland and tribes.

Africans were punished for using their own native language and culture that could not be degraded or stigmatized by their slave masters. They were forced to use broken or old English. Learning and reading was first discouraged and later prohibited by law after Nat Turner used the Bible to lead a slave revolt. Under the rubrics of slavery, Africans were psycho-socially conditioned to despise themselves. Self-hatred and racial disunity was both encouraged and rewarded (Ibid). Self-love, empathy and cooperation among slaves faced severe sanctions or punishments.

Breaking the Slave

The system of slavery was particularly cruel and brutal (Stampp, 1965). The brutality of slavery was evident in physical, psychological and sexual exploitation of the slave. Slaves were subjected to whippings (See Image 58), mutilation, torture, murder, overwork and deprivation of food, clothing and shelter. Slaves were subjected to psychological brutality which included daily humiliation, denial and deformation of their culture, history and humanity (Karenga, 1989).

Image 58: Slave Labor as the Foundation of Wealth in America

Source: www.sjsapush.com

The purpose of the brutality was to objectify the slave; reducing him/her to an object of labor and using his/her "race" as proof their status at the bottom of the human species. Slave women, men and children were subjected to sexual lust and exploitation from their master, his family and white overseers. The principal forms of sexual abuse and brutality were "breeding" and rape (Ibid). Sexual brutality, further dehumanized African-Americans throughout enslavement and afterward until they achieved voting rights. With such rights, under siege today, African-Americans could elect law officials and judges and hold them accountable for their safety from such brutality.

A major aspect of American slavery was its cultural genocide against Africans. This meant the wholesale intentional destruction of their cultural identity and culture itself to produce, reproduce and escalate. This imposed cultural genocide includes the destruction of (1) political identities and ethnic units and identities; (2) families; and (3) cultural leaders. This purge wipes away all units of the preservation and transmission of African culture. It weakens units of real and potential resistance – on cultural and physical level. Cultural genocide nearly destroyed their humanity (Ibid).

The resulting product faced the most brutal and extensive slavery in the history of mankind. Its mechanisms of control consisted of (1) laws; (2) coercive bodies; (3) the church; (4) divisive political strategies; and (5) plantation punishments. Under the laws of slavery, a slave was prohibited from (1) making a contract; (2) testifying against anyone except another African; (3) Using self-defense to protect himself and family members from whites; (4) leaving a plantation without permission; (5) possess firearms; (6) visit and entertain whites and free Africans, particularly in their quarters; (7) assemble without a white person; (8) learn or be taught to read or write; and (9) beat drums or blow horns (Franklin, 1974; Karenga, 1989).

These slave laws were converted into Black Codes after the Civil War into the 21st century and used as means and motives to render civil and criminal laws inequitably. Inequitable application and sentencing applied to the descendants of slaves would lead to the highest incarceration rate in the world (See Image 59). According to Malcolm X this continuous racial mistreatment represents "the yoke of slavery." According to this theory, the slave trade and its "peculiar institution" took Africans away from their freedom and humane treatment in democratic tribal units. Families were torn asunder, divested of their culture and high civilization and became products of tyranny and extensive brutality. Their women were sexually desecrated and the men were emasculated. The "yoke of slavery" persist in discriminatory practices instituted by the white majority at both the individual and institutional levels (Epps, 1991).

Image 59: Incarceration

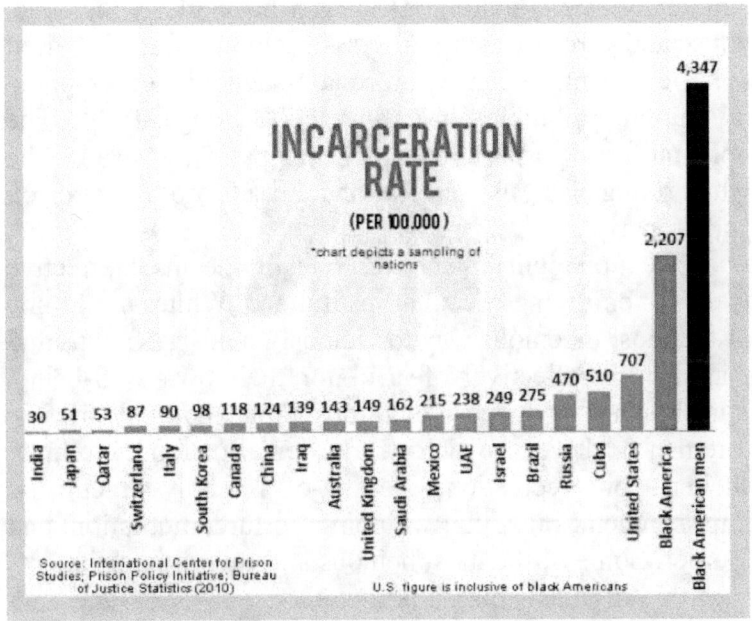

To enforce its suppression of the human rights of the enslaved Africans, the "peculiar institution," and succeeding Jim Crow systems used numerous coercive bodies at local, county, state and federal levels. The coercive bodies included armed federal forces, soldiers, militias, patrols and vigilante committees dedicated to enforcing the "Slave

Codes." In addition, the Church was used as an integral part of the mechanism used to reinforce the "peculiar institution" and its suppression of the human rights of Africans, both enslaved and free (Bennett, 1975). Besides upholding the law, the Church's teachings directly supported the subordination and dehumanization of Africans.

Another machinery of control used by the "peculiar institution" was the use of political, divisive strategies designed to "divide and conquer." Consciousness would be splintered. Unity would be disrupted and undermined to maintain the Master-slave relationship and its race-based hegemony. The strategies included imposing "class" or stratum divisions among Africans who work in the field, house and yards of their masters. Escalating strata was used to stifle dissent, spread disinformation and primarily nipping revolutionary thinking in its infancy (Karenga, 1989). The only uniform purpose was to be empathetic towards the white ruling class, its concerns and the safety of their person and property.

Plantation punishment was one of the most effective means of enforcing "peculiar institution." Whites used some of the most ingenious way to viciously punish Africans and make them collectively fearful for their own well-being. Punishments included demotions from house Africans, foremen or drivers to field work; denial of food, clothing, shelter, or recreation; selling-off family members; imprisonment; branding; whipping; torture; mutilation; and murder. Some of the most heinous and savage punishments used on Africans who would not accept or follow the laws and rules of the slave system include washing wounds in salt and allowing dogs to maul these insurgents. In some instances, slaves were forced to eat worms for failing to pick enough tobacco leaves (Stampp, 1965).

White planters and government officials sanctioned the most repressive and bestial force imaginable to maintain the slave regime. Uncooperative slaves were subjected to having their limbs cut off and being branded. Plantation overseers used a variety of tortures that included chaining, shackling, small maximum security cells without light, fastening a weight to a slave's foot, castration, amputation of feet or limbs, forcing gunpowder into the anus or vagina of a slave and burying them in dirt up to their necks. Other tortures used to break their resistance and to terrorize other slaves included smearing their heads with sugar, so flies and ants would devour them and forcing slaves to eat excrement from animals and humans. For the slaves who threatened their well-being and holdings, slaveholders would roast them barbeque-style over hot coals or an open fire. But the most popular form of labor discipline was the whip or lash. Few slaves escaped this punishment. The use of the rawhide lash symbolized the master's power to punish. Many slaveholders enjoyed the torture of their chattel (Ibid).

Slave masters reared slaves with their eyes on their marketability. This meant seeking more value by whatever means was possible. Massive evidence suggests that many slave masters considered fertile Negro women as an asset and encouraged them to bear children as rapidly as possible. Sexual promiscuity was tolerated, fostered and virtually promoted (Ibid). Some slave marriages were voided if the slave master suspected that either the male or female was sterile. Southern whites promoted the centrality of slave breeding to the accumulation of profits. Black women who bore more than six children were rewarded with gifts, privileges and time off (Gutman, 1975).

When slaves did not reproduce in sufficient numbers, many masters took matters in their own hands. Black women were expected to produce wealth for their masters. For profit and pleasure, black women were constantly subjected to physical and sexual assault by their masters and his white overseers. In the context of American slavery, black women were reduced to the lowest level of biological existence. The rape (See Image 60), an animal-like act, would symbolize the effort to conquer the black women. For the aggressive, repressive and neurotic white males, the black women's vagina was his private property. Raping the black woman was in his eyes comparable to plowing up fertile ground. It was used to break the resistance of the black male who could not protect her (Davis, 1972).

As chattels, Africans were a privately owned commodity. Marriages of blacks on slave masters' or white neighbors' property were tolerated by some masters. When confronted with the inevitable economic downturns that are a permanent feature of capitalism, even the most "humane" master would disrupt the black families by selling off spouse or several children. Obviously, it was not always good business to keep families together. Viewed as prime field hands, children over the age of fourteen were routinely taken from their mothers and fathers (Marable, 1983).

Image 60: Portrait of the Gang Rape of a Slave Woman

Source: www.wikimedia.org/FileChristiaen_von_Couwenbergh_-_Three_Young_White_Men_and_a_Black_Woman

The intersectional sales of slaves prompted one of the greatest migrations in world history and the wholesale decimation of slave families. An estimated 835,000 African-American slaves were moved from the Upper South to the Lower South between 1790 and 1860. The majority an estimated 575,000 were transported between 1830 and 1860. One percent of the total slave population was sold every year between 1820 and 1860. An estimated 35 to 71 percent of marriage-age black women were sold in the interregional slave trade involuntarily from their husbands or partners and families. The notorious public sales of young black girls above the age of 12 to satisfy the sexual needs of white males were frequent. There was even a market specializing in the sales of black children between the ages of 8 to 12 to pedophiles (Franklin, 1969; Gutman, 1975). Blacks for the majority of the nation's history had no rights which whites were bound to respect as slaves and later as freedmen under the Apartheid restrictions of Jim Crow laws and customs.

The Crucible of the Rapid Development
Of the United States

Slavery accelerated the rapid economic development of the United States, as well as Europe. It served as the springboard for the emergence of modern capitalism. In its wake, slavery and its racism expanded and deepened the underdevelopment of the people of Sub-Sahara Africa. The underdevelopment experience of the black population on the continent precipitated by colonization and in the Americas is the inevitable product of an oppressed population's integration into the world market economy and political system. At every level of employment after emancipation in the Americas, white capitalists accumulated higher profits from black labor than they gained from the labor of whites. The constant expropriation of surplus value from black labor is the heart and soul of America's development (Marable, 1983). Cheap immigrant labor before the New Deal's support of collective bargaining was another invaluable source. Today the source of cheap labor and capital accumulation persist from outsourcing jobs to Third World nations like Mexico, China and India.

Initiated during the enslavement of Africa through the present some 150 years after emancipation, the aesthetics and popular culture of white hegemony constantly reinforce the image of the Anglo-Saxon ideal in the minds of blacks, creating the tragic and destructive phenomenon of self-hatred and cultural genocide. The legitimacy of the black experience and its true role in the development of civilization and religion is denied. The illusion that democracy works for everyone regardless of socioeconomic, racial and political background is continually propagated. This norm facilitates a process of cultural genocide which assists the functions of ever-expanding capital accumulation (Ibid).

Slavery is considered a profitable economic system by economists and historians. The use of African slaves offered greater profits than white indentured servants to planters (Whaples, 1995). African slaves had lower economic costs: lack of language barrier once broken and low transportation cost from one state to the other. Higher fertility rates and breeding increased the slave population, the slaveholders' assets, fourfold between 1810 and 1860 after England stopped slave trading from Africa (ICPSR, 2005).

Compared to other assets, slavery was an investment with good returns (Whaples, 1995). Consequently, the emancipation of the slave from bondage would not have ended without the unconditional surrender of the Confederacy to Union forces. By 1860, the rate of return of slavery at the market price was close to 10 percent and rising (Fogel & Engerman, 1995).

The price of slaves rose tremendously in the six decades prior to the War Between the States, even controlling for inflation. Increases in cotton production raised the economic value of slaves. This business relied on the use of slaves to yield high profits. The price of slaves would have increased even more, by at least 50 percent by 1890, if the Civil War had not intervened (Ibid).

The characteristics of the slave, such as sex, age, nature and height were taken into account in the determination of the price of a slave. Males in their mid-twenties were considered the most valuable. At that age, they were judged to be at the peak of their menial productivity and still had a considerable lifespan. The value of slaves with a history of resistance and aggression decreased. Taller males drew higher prices because height was viewed as a proxy for fitness and productivity (Ibid).

A number of pro-slavery sympathizers, like John C. Calhoun, James Henry Hammond and George Fitzhugh, promoted the argument that slavery was "a positive good" for the nation as a whole (Hammond, 1858). Hammond took the lead and presented a speech in the Senate on March 4, 1858, based on his Mudsill Theory. He argued that slaves as the mud-sill of society is the foundation, in which other classes can progress, develop and refine civilization. Blacks do all the menial labor therefore freeing leaders in society to progress (Ibid). Hammond claimed, "Without slavery, blacks would become an insufferable burden to society" (Fitzhugh, 1854; Fishel & Quarles, 1970).

President Lincoln, realized that the Confederacy was solely dependent on the labor of the slaves to produce the agricultural goods needed to continue the war, decided to proclaim that all slaves that fled the plantations and sought refuge behind Union lines would be free. Many left and joined the war effort against the Confederacy. The Union army enlisted at least 180,000. They ended up relieving many of the war-weary union troops. The rebellious South states' arms and supplies were depleted as the Union blocked any trade and commerce for goods needed to continue the fight. South major ally abandoned support for the Confederacy as Emancipation Proclamation and failure at

Gettysburg, PA. They unconstitutional surrender at Appomattox in 1865 ended the war. After a reconstruction period, the nation reunited free of slavery but most of its restrictions on African-Americans prevailed. Intimidation, whippings, lynching and racial segregation continued inhumane treatment for another century.

Environmental Racism as the Legacy of Slavery and the Expendability of Black Lives

Slavery defined blacks as "beast of burden" that are useful in the pursuit of wealth and expendable when freed and seeking to negotiate their own civil and human rights. After slavery, Jim Crow policy of racial segregation was imposed on where blacks lived, employment, business and every social institution. In effect, blacks were ghettoized in the slums with the worse housing and environmental conditions. As urbanization moved most blacks into our oldest cities by the middle of the twentieth-century, environmental racism became a growing concern. The triumphs of the Civil Rights Movement in the 1960s helped the black middle class find improved housing in integrated communities in the suburbs. As the black bourgeoisie took flight, inner-city black communities were repopulated exclusively by the most impoverished people in society. As the residents of the inner-city slums became more exclusively impoverished, environmental racism they faced became a national problem.

Environmental racism is defined as the link between the degradation of the environment and racial demographics of the area being degraded (De La Torre, 2013). The environment is degraded by aged infrastructure, housing, schools, pollution and waste from businesses which have relocated elsewhere. The aged structures emitted lead, pollutants and asbestos to poison and cause life-shorting illnesses. Blacks constitute no less than 16 percent of those suffering from asthma. Multiracials makeup 21 percent of those cases. The neighborhood with the highest documented cases of asthma is the black neighborhood of central Harlem in New York City. Compared to whites, African-Americans had a 35 percent higher rate of this illness. Its cause is triggered by the abundance of insect droppings, mold and mildew found in old housing, as well as diesel, auto and factory pollution along with cigarette smoking (Ibid).

The impact on the life expectancy of African-Americans is deterred by the fact that 68 percent of them live within 30 miles of a coal-fired power plant (Ibid). Here in Florida, it is evident that many blacks live close to a nuclear power plant and are exposed to their incremental leaks of radiation. In addition, most blacks live in close proximity to waste disposal plants that either burn waste for the region or maintain it in landfills which leaked its pollutants into the surrounding black community. Consequently, life expectancy is shortened by at least 10 years. The children have a 500 percent higher death rate from asthma compared to whites. In addition, blacks have a 260 percent higher emergency rate and 250 percent higher hospitalization rate compared to white counterparts (Ibid).

In a racial caste system, blacks are disproportionately impoverished. Race continues to be the most significant variable in determining the location of hazardous waste sites. Poverty heightens the risk of environmental abuse. The economically privileged move away from these sites to avoid these consequences. It is becoming clearer that exposure to toxic waste, aged housing and infrastructure are comparable to lynching a whole person (Ibid). It is also clear that Republicans are adamantly opposed to the continuation of Affordable Health Care to treat and preserve the lives of victims of environmental racism. They are also opposed to most of the regulations needed to control the emissions of pollutants.

References

African-American Registry. (2012). Queen Charlotte. Retrieved January 14, 2012, from www.aaregistry .org

Ajayi, J. F. A., & Epsie, I. (eds). (1972). A thousand years of West African history. New York: Humanities Press.

Ajayi, S. A. (2005). Cheikh Anta Diop. In Kevin Shillington (ed), *Encyclopedia of African History.* New York: Taylor & Francis Group.

al-Athir, A. (2008). The chronicle of Ibn al-Athir for the crusading period from al-Kami fil-Ta'rikh. D. S. Richards (ed.). London: Ashgate Publishing.

Anderson, C. (1994). *Black labor, white wealth: The search for power and economic justice.* Edgewood, MD: Duncan & Duncan, Inc.

Annu, O. (2009, July 28). King Charles Stuart II: The Black Boy King of England. Retrieved April 10, 2016, from www.africaresource.com

Annu, O. (2012, July 11). Dorothea of Denmark, Duchess of Prussia: The Black (Moorish) Europeans. Retrieved March 18, 2016, from www.africaresource.com

_____. (2015, December 8). Bartolome Carranza (1503-1576) Archbishop of Toledo and Primate of Spain: Moorish King of Europe. Retrieved March 19, 2016, from www.africaresource.com

Atlanta Black Star (2015, August 4). 10 European Kings, Queens and Noblemen Who Would Be Considered. Retrieved March 18, 2016, from www.atlantablack star.com

Baker, K. J. (2016, March 12). Make America White Again? Retrieved June 21, 2016, from www.theatlantic.com

_____. (2011, September 20). Gospel According to the Klan: The KKK's Appeal to Protestant America,

1915-1930. Lawrence, KS: University Press of Kansas.

Bergmann, P. M. (1969). *The chronological history of the Negro*. New York: Harper & Row Publishers.

Berry, M. F. (1994, 1971). *Black resistance, white law: A history of constitutional racism in America*. New York: Penguin Group.

Billig, M. (1995). *Banal nationalism*. London: Sage.

Blake, A. (2016, July 22). Former KKK Leader David Duke is Running for Senate. How Well Could He Do? Retrieved July 23, 2016, from www.washington post.com

Botsford, J. (2016, March 7). How Trump Is Inspiring a New Generation of White Nationalists. Retrieved July 30, 2016, from www.huffingtonpost.com

Bowman, M., & Pessin, A. (2014, November 5). Election Gives Republicans Control of US Congress. Retrieved December 12, 2014, from www.voa news.com

Brownstein, R. (2016, June 2). Trump's Rhetoric of White Nostalgia. Retrieved July 30, 2016, from www.atlantic.com

Bump, P. (2016, June 8). Trump Got the Most GOP Votes reifowitzEver – Both For and Against Him – and Other Fun Facts. Retrieved July 30, 2016, from www.washingtonpost.com

Buric, F. (2016, March 11). Trump's Not Hitler, He's Mussolini: How GOP Anti-Intellectualism Created a Modern Fascist Movement in America. Retrieved June 25, 2016, from www.salon.com

Business Day. (2004, October 21). Bush and Kerry Show Opposing Faces of Two Different Americas.

Byrne, D. (2016, February 1). The Echo Chamber. Retrieved August 14, 2016, from www.davidbyrne.com

Chambers, F. (2014, October 20). Democratic Hopefuls Turn on Obama Over His Lackluster Response to the

Ebola Crisis. Retrieved December 12, 2014, from www.dailymail.com

Choma, R. (2016, March 2). Donald Trump's Yooge Flip-Flop on Outsourcing. Retrieved June 22, 2016, from www.motherjones.com

CNN Staff. (2013, July 19). Obama on Trayvon Martin 'That Could Have Been Me.' Retrieved July 19, 2013, from www.cnn.com

Codfried, E. (2011, May 15). Blue Blood is Black Blood (1100-1848). Retrieved March 21, 2016, from www.bluebloodisblackblood.blogspot.com

Davis, A. (1972, Winter-Spring). Reflections on the Black Woman's Role in the Community of Slaves. *The Massachusetts Review*, Vol 13, No.1/ 2, pp. 81-100.

Digital History. (2016). The Middle Passage. Retrieved April 6, 2016, from www.digitalhistory.uh.edu

Dionne, E. (2016, March 14). Trump Cancels Chicago Appearance. Retrieved June 21, 2016, from www.teenvogue.com

Easley, J. (2016, June 7). Trump Campaign Calls Paul Ryan a Racist as Republican Party Burns Itself to the Ground. Retrieved June 23, 2016, from www.politicususa.com

Elliot, E. N. (1969). *Cotton is king and pro-slavery arguments*. New York: Negro Universities Press.

Encyclopedia Britannica. (2016). Vladimir I, Grand Prince of Kiev. Retrieved April 10, 2016, from www.britannica.com

Engel, P. (2001). The realm of St Stephen: A history of Medieval Hungary, 895–1526. New York, NY: I.B. Tauris Publishers.

Engelhardt, T. (2014, November 4). How ISIS and Ebola Took Over the Midterm Elections. Retrieved December 12, 2014, from www.motherjones.com

Epps, A. (1991). *Malcolm X, speeches at Harvard*. New York: Paragon House.

Feldman, N. (2005). *Divided by God*. New York, NY: Farrar, Straus, & Giroux.

Fishel, L. H., & Quarles, B., eds. (1970). The Universal Law of Slavery. *In the Black American: A Documentary History*. Retrieved December 4, 2013, from www.pbs.org

Fitzhugh, G. (1854). Universal Law of Slavery. Retrieved December 4, 2013, from www.pbs.org/wgbh/part4/4h3141t.html

Fogel, R. W. & Engerman, S. L. (1995, 1974). *Time on the Cross: The economics of American Negro Slavery*. New York: W. W. Norton and Company.

Fogel, R. W. (1989). *Without consent of contract: The rise and fall of American slavery*. New York: W. W. Norton and Company.

Follow, B. C. (2015, November 25). Donald Trump's Racist Revival: How the Republican Party Has Given New Life to Unabashed Bigotry. Retrieved June 22, 2016, from www.salon.com

Franklin, J. H. & Moss, Jr., A. A. (2005/1994/1947). *From slavery to freedom: A history of African-Americans*. New York: McGraw Hill, Inc., 1994/1947.

Franklin, J. H. (1988, 1974, 1969). *From slavery to freedom*. New York: Alfred A. Knopf.

Gutman, H. (1975). *Slavery and the numbers game*. Urbana: University of Illinois Press.

Hammond, J. H. (1858). Mudsill Theory. Speech to U. S. Senate, March 14, 1858.

Helderman, R. S., & Hamburger, T. (2016, March 13). Trump Has Profited from Foreign Labor He Says Is Killing U.S. Jobs. Retrieved June 22, 2016, from www.washingtonpost.com

Hinkle, A. B. (2016, March 16). Donald Trump: Trump Enables Racism: Is Giving Racists Carte Blanche. Retrieved June 23, 2016, from www.reason.com

Horwitz, H. (1977). Parliament policy and politics in the reign of William III. Manchester, UK: Manchester University Press.

Hundred Great Black Britons. (2016). Queen Phillipa: England's First Black Queen, Mother of the Black Prince. Retrieved March 20, 2016, from www.100 greatblackbritons.com

ICPSR. (2005, February 25). Historical Demographic, Economic and Social Data: The United States, 1790-1970. *Historical Statistics of the United States.* Retrieved December 4, 2013, from www.umich.edu/ icpsrweb/ICPSR/studies/02896

Irving, C. (2016, June 11). Make America Germany Again. Retrieved June 21, 2016, from www.thedailybeast.com

Jackson, D. (2013, July 19). Obama: Trayvon 'Could Have Been Me.' Retrieved July 19, 2013 from www.usa today.com

Jaide, D. *(2008, January 22). Medieval Europe Before the Advent of the Black Moors of Africa. Retrieved March 16, 2016, from* www.africaresource.com

_____. (2011, November 29). King James IV & I of Scotland & England 1566-1625 and His Daughter. Retrieved April 10, 2016, from www.africaresource. com

_____. (2013, May 13). Vladimir of Kiev, 980-1015: Moorish King of Kiev and Russia. Retrieved April 10, 2016, from www.africaresource.com

_____. *(2015a, December 6). The Swarthy Kings of Europe: Moorish Kings of Europe. Retrieved March 18, 2016, from* www.africaresource.com

_____. *(2015b, December 11). Pope Urban VI. Retrieved March 20, 2016, from* www.africaresource.com

Johnson, A. (2015, September 2). White Nationalism for Trump: The Disturbing Truth About the Donald's Base. Retrieved June 25, 2016, from www.salon.com

176

Judicial Watch. (2014, October 24). JW Exposes Obama's Ebola Plans. Retrieved December 12, 2014, from www.judicialwatch.org/.../w-exposes -obama-ebola-plans

Karenga, M. (1989). *Introduction to black studies*. Los Angeles, CA: University of Sakore Press.

King, T. (2015, December 11). Trump's Grandfather Was a Pimp and Tax Evader; His Father a Member of the KKK. Retrieved June 22, 2016, from www.ahtribune.com

Knox, O. (2013, July 19). Obama: Trayvon Martin 'Could Have Been Me 35 Years Ago.' Retrieved July 19, 2013, from www.usatoday.com

Kosmin, B. A., & Keysar, A. (Eds). (2007). *Secularism & secularity: Contemporary international perspectives*. Hartford, CT: Institute for the Study of Secularism in Society and Culture.

Koutonin, M. (2014, November 1). 100 African Cities Destroyed by Europeans. Retrieved June 24, 2016, from www.siliconafrica.com

Laessig, G. (2011, May 12). Top 20 Achievements of President Obama. Retrieved April 2, 2015, from www.buzzfeed.com

Lay, S. (2015, October 15). Ku Klux Klan in the Twentieth Century. In the *New Georgia Encyclopedia*.

Marable, M. (1983). *How capitalism underdeveloped black America: Problems in race, political economy and society*. Boston, MA: South End Press.

McDaniel, J., & McElwee, S. (2016, March 27). Racial Resentment and the Rise of Donald Trump. Retrieved June 20, 2016, from www.thewpa.wordpress.com

Microsoft's National Broadcasting Corporation. (2016, June 25). MSNBC Live.

Montgomery, P. (2016, March 2). Trump Candidacy Energizes White Supremacists. Retrieved June 23, 2016, from www.huffingtonpost.com

Mullins, P. (2013, January). The Archaeology of Race, Shame and Redemption. Retrieved July 8, 2015, from www.paulmullins.wordpress.com

Obeidallah, D. (2015, August 31). Behind Trump the GOP Really Is Becoming the Racist Party. Retrieved June 23, 2016, from www.thedailybeast.com

Ortiz, G. (2016, June 6). MSNBC's Joe Scarborough Finally Calls Out Donald Trump's Racism After Months of Enabling Him. Retrieved June 23, 2016, from www.americavoice.org

Pager, T. (2016, July 22). GOP's Senate Campaign Arm Condemns David Duke's bid. Retrieved July 23, 2016, from www.politico.com

Parker, C. S. (2016, May 19). Do Trump's Racist Appeal Have a Silver Lining? Retrieved June 20, 2016, from www.prospect.org

Press, B. (2012). *The Obama hate machine: The lies, distortions, and personal attacks on the President- and who is behind them.* New York: St. Martin's Press.

Prowse, D. W. (1896). *A history of Newfoundland: From the English, colonial and foreign records.* London: Eyre & Spottiswoode.

Real History. *(2016). Black Germany: History of the Black Holy Roman Empire. Retrieved March 20, 2016, from* www.realhistoryww.com

_____. (2016). Thirty Years' War. Retrieved June 26, 2016, from www.realhistoryww.com

_____. (2016). *Black Britain. Retrieved April 10, 2016, from* www.realhistoryww.com

Reifowitz, I. (2016, March 28). Trumpism: A Toxic Cocktail of White Racial Resentment, White Cultural Anxiety and White Despair. Retrieved June 20, 2016, from www.huffingtonpost.com

Rodney, W. *(1974). How Europe underdeveloped Africa. Washington, D. C.: Howard University Press.*

Rogers, J. A. *(1972). World's great men of color, I. New York: Macmillan.*

Rosenfeld, S. (2015, July 18). Racism and Xenophobia Are exactly Why Republicans Love Donald Trump, Polls Show. Retrieved June 22, 2016, from www.salon.com

Sala, R. G., & Sala, R. (2013, July, 19). Trayvon Martin Could Have Been Me, Says Obama.' Retrieved July 19, 2013, from http://tv.msnbc.com

Schroeder, P. *(1994). The transformation of European politics, 1763-1848. Glouchester, UK: Clarendon Press.*

Shear, M. D., & Landleroct, M. (2014, October 17). Amid Assurances on Ebola, Obama is Said to Seethe. Retrieved December 12, 2014, from www.nytimes.com

Stampp, K. (1956, 1965). *The peculiar institution: Slavery in the antebellum South.* New York: Vintage.

Taylor, C. (2016, June 21). Busted: Trump Caught Red-Handed Funneling Campaign Cash to His Own Companies. Retrieved June 22, 2016, from www.occupydemocrats.com

Terkel, A. (2016, June 6). Donald Trump Finally Admits His Campaign is Racist. Retrieved June 23, 2016, from www.huffingtonpost.com

Theissen, M. A. (2014, October 27). Ebola and Obama's Crisis of Competence. Retrieved December 12, 2014, from www.washingtonpost. com

Trent. (2014, July 19). Revealed: 5 US Presidents Members of the Racist Cult Ku Klux Klan. Retrieved July 4, 2016, from www.thetrentonline.com

Vaknin, S. (2016, June 1). Is Trump a Fascist! No, Merely a Dangerous Narcissistic Bully. Retrieved June 25, 2016, from www.noisyroom.net

Volsky, I., & Millhiser, I. (2013, July 19). Obama: Trayvon Martin 'Could Have Been Me 35 Years Ago.' Retrieved July 19, 2013, from www.thinkprogress. orgAnderson, C. (1994). *Black labor, white wealth: The search for power and economic justice.* Edgewood, MD: Duncan & Duncan, Inc.

Waldman, P. (2015, November 25). Donald Trump Is Running the Most Explicitly Racist Campaign Since 1968. Retrieved June 22, 2016, from www.theweek.com

Webb, S. S. (1995). *Lord Churchill's coup.* New York: Alfred A. Knopf.

Weber, D. J. *(2009).* The Spanish frontier in North America: The brief edition. New Haven, CT: ale University Press.

Wecker, M. (2015, June 20). History of Dutch Jews role in slavery is bluntly depicted. Retrieved March 12, 2016, from www.forward.com

Whaples, R. (1995, March). Where is There Consensus Among American Economic Historians? The Results of a Survey on Forty Propositions. *Journal of Economic History*, 139-154.

Williams, C. (1974). *Destruction of black civilization: Great issues of race from 4500 B. C. to 2000 A. D.* Chicago, Illinois: Third World Press.

Wecker, M. (2015, June 20). History of Dutch Jews in Slavery Is Bluntly Depicted. Retrieved July 31, 2016, from www.forward.com

Wilson, A. (1990). *Black-on-violence.* New York: Afrikan World Infosystems.

Wilson, B. (2016, May 17). Trump Campaign Tied to Second Leader of White Nationalist Party. Retrieved June 25, 2016, from www.huffingtonpost.com

www.ingramcontent.com/pod-product-compliance
Lightning Source LLC
Chambersburg PA
CBHW060303290526
45789CB00001B/394